Lessons from the Hardwoods

by
R. McKenzie Fisher

New Leaf Press

First printing: April 1996

ISBN: 0-89221-311-6
Library of Congress: 95-72881

Cover by Multnomah Graphics, Portland, Oregon

Photo on pages 13, 51, and 61 courtesy of Tim Umphrey.
Photo on page 28 courtesy of USC.
Photo on page 39 courtesy of the University of North Carolina.
Photo on page 82 courtesy of UCLA.

Presented to:

_____

Presented by:

_____

Date:

_____

Dedication

The more I write, the more I realize how many people have been there for me during this (and all the other books). I especially want to thank:

Ed — for the wonderful gifts of sports books and Microsoft Basketball for our computer. Information overload!!

Brian — for being my personal "Sports Information Service." (How do you keep all that in your head?!)

Mom, Ed's folks, and other family members and friends — for buying all the books and encouraging others to buy even more.

Marsha and Martha — for their prayers about my writing and the distractions that came during this book. What treasured friends!

Greg, Suzanne, Dave, and others at Athletes in Action — for sharing your contacts for our Foreword.

Brent Price — for writing our Foreword and for his great example both on and off the court.

Jesus — for being with me constantly and carrying all my burdens so I would write through difficult times. I praise Your Holy Name!!

Foreword

Everyone knows that passing is one of the most important aspects of the game of basketball. Seldom do you snag a rebound and run full court to slam-dunk the ball. When it does happen, it's exhilarating for both the player and the fans, but ordinarily it takes teamwork, and that means passing the ball from player to player.

Bringing the ball down the court and setting up our pass offenses are my major responsibilities. Nothing is more exciting than passing to our power forward and watching him score for us. An alley-oop pass is even more fun — not just for us, but for the fans.

There is another area in my life where passing has meant a lot to me as well. I was blessed to grow up in a Christian home where my parents passed their faith along to me. However, just as in basketball, you have to be prepared to catch the ball — you must personally receive Jesus as your Saviour. Your parents' faith will not make you a Christian. I am thankful that I received Christ early in my life and have had the chance to pass that message along to others.

That is what Rita does in this book, *Lessons from the Hardwood.* She passes her faith along to others. When I was first contacted, Rita was still writing the manuscript for the basketball book. I enjoyed reading her baseball book, *Lessons from the Diamond*, and was anxious to see how she would make similar correlation's between the hoop game I love and our daily walk with Christ. She talks about the passing game of basketball in the "Alley-Oop" lesson.

She did a FANtastic job of weaving wonderful stories and illustrations from the game of basketball with other lessons in daily life. I just love it. Who wouldn't? The book is for everyone. Kids can learn some of the basics about how to play better basketball. Those who already understand the game will enjoy taking that knowledge and connecting it to a deeper meaning in their lives. Moms and dads will also enjoy reading it to their young children. The lessons about our spiritual beliefs play a vital role in family life. That is important to me. I hope we can help kids appreciate and respect their families and help parents take responsibility for loving and training their children. More importantly, I hope folks of all ages will learn to let Jesus Christ be their example for how to live in our families and in the world around us.

The books make great gifts for Christians and non-believers alike. If you know someone who likes basketball but doesn't know much about Jesus, giving them *Lessons from the Hardwood* can be your way of passing the faith along!

— Brent Price

Introduction

Loving sports and with my older brother attending the University of Cincinnati during Oscar Robertson's final two seasons, was I a basketball fan? You bet! Ironically UC finished only third while "The Big O" played. After his graduation, they won back-to-back NCAA titles in 1961-62. Our parents took me down to the field house on campus when the Bearcats returned for the victory celebration.

I had a more "up close and personal" look at the hard court in high school as a cheerleader for three years. Standing barely outside the boundaries, I had to be careful to lead cheers and not be heard second-guessing the refs. Someone should have told me that "Are you blind?" is not a cheer!

I would continue to disagree with the officials when our son played hoopball in school. I was never demeaning or crass in my remarks, but it became a running joke with Brian and his friends. They came down after one game to watch the video Ed had just taken. Suddenly they were rewinding — not to watch themselves on a specific play but to hear what I had yelled at the ref. Needless to say, I changed my ways. I sat far enough away from Ed at the games that the recorder couldn't pick up my voice!

Seriously, as a parent booster (better known as an "Eagle Mom"), I had a great time getting to know Brian's teammates. During their freshman year, I took mini-pizzas and sports drinks for them to chow down during their after-school study hall prior to 4:00 p.m. games. (Better nourishment than what the candy and pop machines had to offer.) By the time the boys made varsity, I was writing mini-poems on labels for "Big Red" gum and making 20-foot posters with slogans for parents to unroll along the highway route the team bus took to an away game. We delivered "Eagle-grams" and balloons to the kids' homes, met the team bus coming back from an away game with a welcome home cordon of headlights from our cars, and hosted special team dinners on the nights prior to big rivalries. We even decorated the team bus with black balloons, wore special "Coach is 40!" name tags and got the opponent's announcer to wish our varsity coach a "Happy Over-the-Hill Birthday"!

Perhaps my favorite spirit idea was making each player his own "Breakfast of Champions trophy." Cutting carefully around individual pictures, I glued each photo onto a single-serving-size box of Wheaties. (See photo with Lesson 15.) They continue to be conversation pieces with first-time visitors. Little kids ask Brian (and the others), "WOW! How did you get on a Wheaties box?"

We don't have to be real champions in basketball or any sport to feel special in life. Christ accepts us just as we are and loves us no matter what! That is what real victory is all about — knowing Him, accepting His death for us, and allowing His Spirit to guide us in our daily lives. I hope as we share these lessons about both basketball and everyday life, you will come to know Him better and receive His unconditional love.

In His Love,
Rita McKenzie Fisher

Lesson 1
The Perfect Substitute

What do Anthony Mason, Dell Curry, Cliff Robertson, and Bill Walton have in common? Each earned the NBA's "Sixth Man" Award. With five starting players on a basketball team, the "sixth man" is the best substitute off the bench. The NBA has awarded such outstanding play since 1982-83 when Bobby Jones (Philadelphia) won the honor.

Playing only 31 minutes per game, Kevin McHale came off Boston's bench for an average of 18.4 points and 7.4 rebounds to help lead the Celtics to the NBA championship in 1984. He was the NBA "Sixth Man" both that year and the following season. In 1985-86 McHale became a starting forward, but the team's bench kept the award. Bill Walton, acquired from the Clippers and coming off serious foot injuries, played in 80 games for the Celts. While in for only a little over 19 minutes per game, he averaged 7.6 points, 6.8 rebounds, 2 assists, and one blocked shot.

Other winning NBA super subs have been Roy Tarpley and Eddie Johnson. Ricky Pierce and Detlef Schrempf each won the award twice. Who do you think deserves the Sixth Man Award this year?

College hoops don't give an award, but having talented back-up off the bench is a key for teams making it to the Final Four. From the start, Rob Pelinka's role was "sixth man" for Michigan as they won the NCAA championship his freshman year. During his junior and senior seasons (1991-92 and 1992-93), the "Fab Five" (all-freshman, all-starting, all-stars) arrived. Pelinka again came off the bench to help those teams, both seasons ending with a loss in the NCAA Championship game. While there was no "sixth man" award, Pelinka graduated with a 3.9 GPA in business and was Academic All-Big-Ten two years in a row.

Prior to the 1995 NCAA Championship game, UCLA's leading point guard Tyus Edney was injured. CBS analyst Billy Packer said. "Without Edney, UCLA will face 94 feet and 40 minutes of trouble against the Arkansas pressing defense." Said Packer of substitute Cameron Dollar's slow start, "See, that's what I was talking about. They can't expect Dollar to come off the bench and replace Edney." However, Dollar played 36 minutes, stripped the ball from the Razorbacks at a prime moment, had 4 steals, 8 assists, and 6 points in the 89-78 Bruin victory.

The depth of the bench is vital for success in basketball (or any other team sport). Second and third-string players push the starters during practice and are ready to jump in at any moment — being fully prepared to do their best.

If you are "sixth" (or even seventh or eighth) on your team, don't put yourself down. You are an important part of the team. And if you are a starter, don't let the "big head" keep you from appreciating your team-mates on the bench.

In some situations in life we may be asked to lead. In other places we are the substitutes. Where can God use you to fill in for someone else? What about being a Big Brother or Big Sister to a child without many role models? If you are older there may be young families in your neighborhood or church who live away from their loved ones. Perhaps you could be an "adopted grandparent." Teenagers can reverse the situation and "adopt" an older neighbor and volunteer to help

10

around the yard or just spend time together.

The most important substitute in history came when God sent His only Son, Jesus, to take the place for all of us. Through God's mercy and grace, Christ took our sins upon his shoulders and bled and died on the cross that we might have a "true adoption" back into God's family. Don't let His suffering go unrewarded. If you haven't already, repent of your sins, and accept Christ as Your Saviour today.

"He [Christ] personally carried the load of our sins in his own body when he died on the cross, so that we can be finished with sin and live a good life from now on" (1 Pet. 2:24;LB).

"I entered the Arkansas game wearing a 'Jesus is the Reason' wristband as a reminder to focus on Jesus Christ and let my God-given abilities take over. I don't worry about filling anyone's shoes, because I play for Jesus Christ." — Cameron Dollar

Note of interest: Dollar and Pelinka have more in common that having been successful "sixth" men. They are both committed Christians who have been featured in the Christian magazine *Sports Spectrum*.

Lessons 2

Success

"It's always been very simple to me how the game of basketball should be played. Score on offense. Stop the other team on defense." says Dr. J. He goes on, "Prepare before the game, celebrate the victories, and learn from the losses."

During the decade of the sixties, Boston Celtics did a lot of celebrating, and everyone else should have learned a lot. During 13 years (1957-69), the Celts won 11 NBA titles. Only the St. Louis Hawks (1958) and the Philadelphia 76ers (1967) broke through the Boston dynasty. Second behind Boston's 16 titles is the Lakers' record with 6 while in LA and another 5 from years in Minnesota.

"Winning it all" and owning that title "ring" seems to be the definition of success to many. But what about all of those great players of the sixties who didn't play for Boston? What about some of the great All-Stars of the modern era who have yet to earn a ring? Some lesser-skilled bench players for the Bulls, Rockets, and Pistons (the only teams to win in the nineties to date) have the jewelry. But does that make their careers more successful?

One NBA Hall of Famer (1979), Jerry West, refused to quit until he won a ring. Being considered second only to Oscar Robertson at the guard position during his era and owning an Olympic gold medal (1960) wasn't enough for West. Neither was being only the third player in NBA history to reach 25,000 points. During 13 of his 14 seasons the Lakers would miss the Finals only four times and lose 8 of 9 to the Celtics during

Hakeem Olajuwon
Houston Rockets

their 1960s run. In 1969 West was named MVP of the Championship series, the only member of a losing team to ever garner the award. "He took a loss harder than any player I've ever known," says Laker broadcaster Chick Hearn. Prior to the 1971-72 season he considered retirement, but when Wilt Chamberlain was traded to the Lakers, West decided to stay on board. They won the title that season and he played for two more years, retiring with many records and the coveted ring. West later coached the Lakers for three years and become their general manager.

Len Rosen, agent for such stars as Magic Johnson, says of West, "For him, it's all about winning. And he knows what it takes to win." Rosen continues, "It's not about money. He's not afraid to take a chance. Not every decision works out, but if it's not a good decision, he just lives with it and moves on."

That is a lesson for all of us in the successes and failures of life. In *Growing Strong in the Seasons of Life* Chuck Swindoll says, "The person who succeeds is not the one who holds back, fearing failure, nor the one who never fails . . . but rather the one who moves on in spite of failure."

We can't always control situations that cause us to fail. Sometimes we can try our best and still others are better. Often plans fail for unknown reasons. None of that should stop us. As Dr. J says, we can learn from our losses. Remember, the only time you fail is the last time you try!

"Be strong and very courageous . . . careful to obey the law Moses gave you . . . that you may be successful wherever you go" (Josh. 1:7).

"There's only two things in the NBA. There's winning and there's misery." — Pat Riley (NBA coach — Lakers, Knicks, Heat)

Lesson 3
Assists

Charles Barkley slams the ball through the hoop to the cheers of exhilarated Suns' fans. He points at KJ, his teammate Kevin Johnson. This isn't a disparaging "finger in your face" gesture. It's his "Thank you" or "You made it happen"— a way to share the glory. Assists have now gained status as a part of the game of basketball.

1995 Co-Rookie-of-the-Year Jason Kidd had 25 assists with the Mavericks on February 8, 1996 — only 5 short of (Bullets) Scott Skiles' NBA single game record. However, neither will be known as the Assist King. That title clearly belongs to John Stockton of the Utah Jazz. He led the 1994-95 season, averaging 12.3 assists per game for a total of 1,011. NJ Nets star Kenny Anderson was second with 680. At the end of the 1994-95 season, Stockton had 7 seasons of over 1,000 assists and 8 titles in a row. During the following season Stockton surpassed Magic Johnson and Oscar Robertson to become the all-time assist leader in the NBA.

One of the classic assists in the game is the well-executed pick-and-roll. Even when the defense knows it's coming, it's still a most dependable scoring play. "The pick-and-roll is the play you run right after 'The Star Spangled Banner,' " says Charlotte Hornet assistant coach John Bach, known as a defensive guru. The ball handler steers the defender into the blockade (or pick) which is set by the big man. The ball handler then maneuvers around the pick to an open spot on the court. As soon as the defense commits to him, the ball is then smoothly passed to the big teammate moving toward the hoop.

"Watch any game and you will see it repeatedly," according to Sports Illustrated columnist Phil Taylor. "A player sets a pick for the dribbler and then rolls to an open spot, looking for a return pass and an easy basket." Taylor says that the play works best with a small, clever guard and an imposing big man. Examples he gives of successful pick-and-roll duos: Bob Cousy and Bill Russell from the old Boston Celtic dynasty; Isaiah Thomas and Bill Laimbeer from the 1980s Pistons; and today's John Stockton and Karl Malone from the Jazz. Cousy himself says of this pair, "Malone comes out and sets that big pick and Stockton handles the ball like a world-class violinist." When asked how he knows when to make his move, Malone answers, "It's just a feeling you get." There is a shared excitement in the success of this play as with all assists.

It's great that the NBA finally recognizes assists as an honored category. It does involve sacrifice on the part of the assisting player in a game where high-point-man has been regarded as the star in the past.

Making sacrifices should be a recognized part of our Christian lives as well. Being the "star" is not our goal but being able to help others in their time of need.

Paul Crouch shares about the founding of TBN (Trinity Broadcasting Network) in 1973. During the telethon to fund the station's start-up, a missionary couple, home on furlough from New Guinea where they had worked in the "disease and mosquito infested jungles," decided to donate the balance of their travel check to the cause.

Crouch said he found it hard to accept the generous check. But Brother Farnsworth insisted. "Paul, God told me to do this; I have to obey the Lord. You have to take it!"

Crouch believes the reason God has so richly blessed TBN
is because the "precious seed has been planted by faithful servants of
God who gave sacrificially like the Farnsworths."

What are we sacrificing for the Lord's work? Perhaps it's money we
have planned to use for a vacation or a new car. How committed are we
to the church building program or the social concerns mission project?
Maybe it's time or effort that we are being asked to sacrifice. Maybe it's
using the talent God has richly bestowed on us.

Sacrifice is defined as "to forfeit one thing for another considered to
be of greater value." What is it of yours that God can use for a greater
cause?

"Nobody should seek his own good, but the good of others" (1 Cor. 10:24).

"Give my teammates a lot of credit. I wouldn't have that many assists if
they weren't making the baskets." — Jason Kidd (2/8/96)

Lesson 4
In the Spotlight

Imagine it's your first NBA game, and it's nationally televised. You hear the cheering fans and your heart begins to pump faster. You lead the team onto the court for the pre-game warm-ups. As you go for your first professional lay-up, you suddenly find yourself lying face down on the floor. In the excitement of dressing, you somehow overlooked tightening the drawstring of your warm-up pants. They have fallen around your ankles, tripping you and causing you to stumble in front of an arena of expectant fans and the entire viewing world. That was the Los Angeles introduction of Earvin Johnson. "Everybody was there to see me play in my first game," Magic recalled, "and it turned out to be my most embarrassing moment." He recovered well, scoring 26 points in the Laker victory that night (10/12/79) to begin a stellar NBA career.

Magic can be thankful it was in the era before today's pre-game fanfare with its pounding music, cloaked darkness pierced by sudden spotlights and indoor fireworks as local announcers stretch out each syllable of every player's name. What else could you expect when Disney's Mickey Mouse lives next door to the Orlando Magic! Some point to the Chicago Bulls as originators, but this energy-packed atmosphere traces back to the Harlem Globetrotters. Strains of *Sweet Georgia Brown* conjure up visions of their ball handling maneuvers and clown-like yet sharpshooting abilities to anyone who has ever watched them at courtside or on TV.

There's nothing wrong with a little added excitement and music. Phoenix Suns forward Wayman Tisdale combines his love of basketball and music to delight fans. He wrote the theme song for the Suns and has played his bass guitar at Jam Session festivities (that's not the Slam-Dunk Contest) during the All-Star weekend. His Motown jazz album *Power Forward,* is not a Christian album per se, but does have a cut of "Amazing Grace" and other spiritual songs. "People can tell," says Tisdale. "You get the message."

Tisdale believes people see a difference in him when he performs whether on the court or onstage. He hopes they think, *No matter what the situation, he always seemed to shine. There's a player who loves the Lord.*

We all need to "let our light shine" and to remember that the real Light of the World is Jesus (Matt. 5:14-15; John 8:12).

In his book *The Wounded Heart* Dr. Dan Allender tells us that "dark secrets" forced on us in the past cause shame, and lead to many forms of mental illness and poor physical health. Now we are too embarrassed to tell anyone because we are sure if we do, they will never love us. That is not true. God loves us no matter what, and He fully understands.

David Seamands also understands. After almost 50 years as a Christian counselor, pastor, teacher, and author, Seamands has seen what kind of damage this shame and secrecy causes. He says, "We try to keep things covered up so we don't have to face the truth or see what the light will reveal." He goes on to explain, "When God shines the crossbeams of His light into the dark caves and graves of our lives, it is not so He can find out something about us He doesn't already know. Perhaps it is so that we can find out something about ourselves *we* may not know, or may not even want to know. . . . We can allow His grace and love to enter that hidden, hurting area of our lives" in order to heal us.

Let God's light shine in your heart to heal your worst pain. Then, let His Light shine through you to reach out into the darkness around you and touch others with His healing love.

"If we walk in the light, as he is in the light, we have fellowship with one another, and the blood of Jesus Christ, his Son, purifies us from all sin" (1 John 1: 7).

"I feel very blessed that the Lord gave me two talents that can reach millions of people. I can reach a certain amount of people through basketball, and musically even that many more. I want to use those to the best of my ability to glorify God." — Wayman Tisdale

Lesson 5
Babes of the Court

A month after his high school prom, 19-year-old Kevin Garnett was the #5 pick in the 1995 NBA draft. A headline in *The Sporting News Pro Yearbook* read: "Thrown to the Wolves." Former Celtic star, now VP of operations for the Minnesota Timberwolves, Kevin McHale says, "There are going to be some tough times ahead for him. We're just going to be there for him in every way we can to help."

More common in baseball and hockey, only four other players had jumped straight from high school to the professional ranks in basketball: Moses Malone (1974), Darryl Dawkins (1975), Bill Willoughby (1975), and Shawn Kemp (1989).

Underclassmen coming out of college programs is another consideration. Coaches and schools spend a lot of time and money recruiting valuable athletes, groom them for a year or two, and are left "holding the ball" without these stars, as NBA dollar signs beckon. Ten underclassmen were selected in the first round of the '95 draft (including four sophomores who went ahead of Garnett.) NCAA powerhouse North Carolina lost two of its starters — Jerry Stackhouse (76ers) and Rasheed Wallace (Bullets) — the first two undergrads to leave Dean Smith's program since Michael Jordan left following his junior year.

Georgia Tech coach Bobby Cremins is not too concerned, "If we lose a great player . . . go get another great player." He believes there is enough talent in the college-bound pool for NCAA basketball to remain competitive. Cremins does care that some kids might get in over their heads. "If a kid is physically and emotionally ready to go, that's fine," he said, "but it's so hard to tell."

Who can blame the kids for taking the money? What if they get injured while they wait? While "education will never hurt you" may be true, isn't part of a college education to obtain a more secure job? Maybe basketball isn't that secure, but if these players invest their money wisely, they should be set for life. They certainly need sound financial advice and family support as they make the difficult transition from teenager to wealthy celebrity.

Dr. J (Julius Erving), who left college himself after three years, expresses this concern: "Players today have trouble relating to the longevity and historical perspective of the game because of the economics. It's get in, make the money, and then get out." Michael Jordan agrees, "The love of the game is what it's all about, not what it provides. I think today's athletes love the game for what it provides, not for what it is!"

These young men need the guidance of hoop statesmen like Dr. J and MJ. We can only hope there are enough McHales in the NBA navy to stand by these "babes of the court."

Standing by and praying for "babes in Christ" is a responsibility we all share, and this often has little to do with age. We obviously need to be faithful to the children (our own and others). We can teach them in Sunday school and Vacation Bible School programs — and more importantly set loving examples of Christ in our homes.

Adults of all ages also come to know Christ for the first time in their lives. We need to accept them non-judgmentally and nurture them as they learn and grow. We can help them through Bible studies, mentorships, and through our various church programs. If you are a "babe" yourself, seek the nurture and support you need.

Missionary Peter Marshall offered this prayer: "As we grow to maturity, our faith is blighted with doubts, withered with worry, tainted with sophistication. We pray Thou will make us like children again — not childish, but childlike in the simplicity of a faith that is willing to trust Thee."

May we always be childlike — not childish — both in our faith and in all walks of life.

"Like newborn babies, crave pure spiritual milk, so that by it you may grow up in your salvation" (1 Pet. 2:2).

"The physical capabilities of a player 19 or 20 can parallel those of college seniors, but the difference is maturity. Part of that is the ability, day-to-day, to make good, professional decisions. That's hard enough for mature people to do." — Dr. J (Hall of Fame 1992)

Lesson 6
Standing Tall among Giants

Playing basketball in 1942, Bob Kurland found himself at a disadvantage — he was too tall! Kurland recalled, "The six-footers were faster and more poised" and coaches weren't giving taller guys a chance. Finally accepted at Oklahoma A&M (now Oklahoma State), Kurland (6'10-1/2") was the first to block shots on their way down into the basket. Goaltending was added to the rules after his sophomore year. He was also adept at tip-ins and playing "above the rim" for what would later be known as "the dunk." Averaging 17.1 and 19.5 points respectively, Kurland led Oklahoma A&M to two national titles in 1945-46 and was inducted into the Hall of Fame in 1961.

Being a giant is no longer a disadvantage in basketball. Look at the center post in any NBA game. Gheorghe Muran of the Bullets stands at 7'7". Not far behind are Shawn Bradley (7'6"), Rik Smits (7'4"), Dikembe Mutombo (7'2"), David Robinson, Shaquille O'Neal and Vlade Divac, (all at 7'1") and Hakeem Olajuwon and Patrick Ewing (both at a mere 7'0").

During the 1995-96 season, there were 45 NBA players over 7 feet and only 10 under 6 feet tall. Remember the biblical account of David and Goliath? Just as the "little guy" won that victory, there are some equally successful stars on the shorter side in the NBA.

Spud Webb (5'7") led the NBA in free throw percentage (93.4) in 1994-95 hitting 226 of 242 shots from the line. Webb also proved you don't have to be a giant to jam during the 1986 All Star celebration when he stole the slam-dunk show from the taller court men, ousting among others, Hawks' teammate Dominique Wilkins.

At 5'3" Muggsy Bogues is also a leader in the tall man's arena standing fifth in both free throw percentage (88.9) and assists (8.7 per game) during 1994-95. In his first eight seasons in the NBA, he had over 100 steals per year and dished out over 600 assists in each of the first seven seasons. Drafted by Washington in 1987, Bogues was "a curiosity, a way to sell a few more tickets" according to sportswriter Ron Green. Traded to the Charlotte Hornets, Bogues now runs the show for their on-court drives. "When you're playing against the Hornets, you're always thinking Larry Johnson and Alonzo Mourning are the team leaders," says former teammate Hersey Hawkins, "but then you find our Muggsy Bogues is the heart and soul."

Another small guard with a big heart is Avery Johnson. Listed in San Antonio's media guide at 5'11", he averaged 16.2 points and 7.5 assists per game in the play-offs against the eventual 1995 NBA Champion Rockets. Spurs GM Gregg Popovich says, "Johnson epitomizes a floor leader, gets everyone involved and is always under control."

Getting people involved off the court is another way Johnson leads. Hosting a dinner for over 100 needy families in the San Antonio area, A.J. served food and shared one-on-one with each kid. "I want him to know that he's blessed and to share these blessings with him," says A.J. He believes it is his responsibility to work hard and support others both on and off the court. "Why can't I go out here and give my best out on a basketball court for 48 minutes AND make a difference in the lives of people?" asks

Johnson rhetorically. "That's how my NBA career is going to be measured."

What a great measuring rod! Size has nothing to do with what God calls us to do. What about helping out at a homeless shelter or soup kitchen? Does your local church have a clothing cupboard for the needy? Why not help start one?

USA Today and the Points of Light Foundation (started by former President George Bush) sponsor an annual "Make a Difference Day." Youth groups, families, communities, and individuals are challenged to find creative ways of reaching out to others. One of the 1995 judges, TV host Kathie Lee Gifford suggests, "Go to a facility and rock a child. Adopt an elderly person. Visit a shut-in." She reminds us that "these things don't cost a lot of money, but are priceless."

"As the body without the spirit is dead, so faith without deeds is dead" (James 2:26).

"I will coach many, many years, but I don't know if I will ever coach a man with the professionalism and determination of Avery Johnson." — Bob Hill (San Antonio Spurs Coach)

Lesson 7

Look Out, Boys!
Here We Come!

"THESE DAYS Little Girls don't live down THE LANE. They DRIVE down it." This State Farm Insurance ad sponsors Rebecca Lobo, Sheryl Swoopes, Lisa Leslie, Teresa Edwards, and other members of the 1996 USA Women's National Basketball Team. Their style of play depicts a new era of basketball history quite different from the first female game played at Smith College in 1893.

Senda Berenson Abbott (a Smith instructor) and Clara Baer (Newcomb College, New Orleans) each wrote to Dr. James Naismith for information about his "new game." Misunderstanding the diagrams, Abbott developed rules with each team divided into three offensive and three defensive players, allowing each set to play only half-court. This six-on-six version was finally dropped in the late 1960s for the five-player full-court game. (Abbott was selected to the Hall of Fame in 1984.)

In 1972 federally mandated Title IX laws forced the NCAA to offer more women's sports. Women's basketball became an Olympic event in 1976. Since the first women's NCAA Final Four in 1982, televised coverage has increased to several weekly games. Both participation and fan popularity have grown. Over 4.7 million spectators saw women's collegiate games in 1992-93. Fans regularly filled the Pavilion to watch the 1994-95 University of Connecticut Lady Huskies run through their

Cheryl Miller
University of Southern California

perfect 35-0 season, capturing the NCAA crown. Beating out tennis star Monica Seles, UConn's Lobo was named the 1995 Associated Press Female Athlete of the Year.

Lobo may have the chance to join Seles as a professional athlete in the near future. A group headed by Steve Hams and five other private investors are forming an 8-team American Basketball League for women. Hoping to build on the publicity generated by the 1996 Olympics, the ABL has already signed most of the US team to its new franchises which will begin play in 1997. To ensure parity, two top players will be assigned to each team based on their regional popularity. The remaining roster spots will be filled from open tryouts and an inaugural draft from top college females.

These gals, however, will not be the first to play pro basketball. Nancy Lieberman (College Player of the Year in both 1979 and 1980) and others were a part of the short-lived Women's Professional Basketball League (1978-83). Lieberman also played with the Washington Generals (touring opponents for the Harlem Globetrotters) where she met and married teammate Tim Cline. In 1993 Nancy and three other women won the Hoop It Up world title. Lieberman-Cline was inducted into the Basketball Hall of Fame in 1996.

She is disheartened that young girls do not know the history of those who led them onto the court. "It's men perpetuating men; they make them [male stars] legendary," says Lieberman-Cline. "We don't have the resources in women's sports to promote the legends . . . like Lucy Harris (Hall of Fame 1991), Nancy Dunkle, Carol Blazejowski (H/F 1993), Annie Meyers (H/F 1992), Cheryl Miller and Carolyn Bush-Roddy."

Perhaps we all should take a look at these legends and other Hall of Famers in order to better appreciate the great strides that have been made in women's basketball. Lieberman also found another group whose heritage she began to appreciate. During her freshman year at Old Dominion (1976), she became a Christian through contact with Athletes in Action.

Athletes in Action, Fellowship of Christian Athletes, Campus Crusade and other similar groups are touching lives daily with God's love. Many former college and professional stars give their time and support to these efforts — helping with clinics, attending banquets, playing on teams for fund raising events, and most of all, sharing their personal testimonies with youth (and adults) around them.

You may want to invite one of these groups into your school or have your business help sponsor a camp for youth in your community. If you have played college ball (in any sport) you might even want to consider becoming a part of their team.

We can all be a part of God's team by spreading His Word, by leading others to Christ, and by setting an example of His love to those around us.

"For through what Christ has done, he has triumphed over us so that now wherever we go he uses us to tell others about the Lord and to spread the gospel like a sweet perfume" (2 Cor. 2:14;LB).

"So often kids today think the game started with them. It's important to share the stories about the great women who have played this game." — Nancy Lieberman-Cline (youngest member on the 1976 silver medal US Olympic team)

Lesson 8
Color Blind

Perhaps no where else do we see a better color-blind atmosphere than on the basketball court. While inter-racial play is an important part of many sports today, none perhaps has the intensity and unity of purpose as the game of hoops.

This has not always been the case. Chuck Cooper (Duquesne University) was the first black player drafted in the NBA (by the Celtics) in 1950. Nat "Sweetwater" Clifton actually signed his contract first. Earl Lloyd (West Virginia) was the first black to actually play in a game (with the Washington Capitols) on October 31, 1950 — one day ahead of Cooper and two before Clifton's opening game with the Knicks.

All three were victims of the racism of that era. When he could not stay in the same hotels with the rest of the team, Clifton roomed and spent his free time with the many friends he had made while touring with the Harlem Globetrotters prior to coming to the NBA. Even by the early 1960s, life on the road had not changed. When Oscar Robertson became the first black on the Cincinnati Royals team, he was still not permitted to stay with the team in most cities but had to find housing in college dorms.

The first black head coach in the NBA was Bill Russell, who served as a player-coach for the Boston Celtics from 1967-69 — two NBA title seasons. Ken Hudson was the first black NBA referee, officiating a Bulls-Sixers game in 1968. Georgetown head coach John Thompson was the first black American to lead a college team to the NCAA title in 1984.

Keith Jones was hired as assistant trainer by General Manager Pat Williams with the Orlando Magic in 1988. After a year in the role, he ran into Los Angeles Clipper GM Elgin Baylor in an elevator and found out they were in need of a new head trainer. At 27 Jones became not only the first black, but the youngest trainer in the NBA. "God has been responsible for opening doors for me," says Jones. "All I've had to do is walk through them."

Fred Hickman believes God has opened doors for him as well. While perhaps not the first black sports anchor, Hickman's work on CNN's Sports Tonight began at the tender age of 24 and culminated with a 1994 CableAce Award. Hickman has co-anchored with Nick Charles since 1980. They have broadcast more than 3,000 programs together and are a shining example of what color-blind living should be. They are more than co-workers; they are friends off-the-air as well. They also share deep spiritual beliefs in Christ. "We really bring out the best in each other," says Charles. "We both feel a passion for the Lord, and I think that has united us. I thought we always had rapport, but this goes way beyond that."

Bill McCartney, former head football coach at Colorado and one of the founders of Promise Keepers, believes in that bond through Christ. After the first Promise Keeper conference in 1991 McCartney said he "looked over the crowd and noticed that it was overwhelmingly white. The absence of men of color hit me between the eyes." He said the Spirit of God spoke to him, "You can fill that stadium, but if men of other races aren't there, I won't be there either."

McCartney shares in his book, "Racism is Satan's stronghold. Imagine what a united church could do with the gang problem . . .

with the need for young people in single-parent homes to have positive role models . . . with the lack of educational and employment opportunities in certain segments of our society."

Sounds like a political agenda. Senator Bill Bradley (former NBA star) and former Congressman Jack Kemp (former NFL star) always had a better grasp of the issues dealing with racism than most legislators. Bradley and Kemp received a great deal of understanding from playing sports. Relying on teammates of other races, truly living together while on the road, and developing inter-racial friendships are lessons from athletics that we all need to learn for unity in our communities and the world.

"There is neither Jew nor Greek, slave nor free, male nor female, for you are all one in Christ Jesus" (Gal. 3:28).

"They used to call what we played 'ghetto ball.' Now guys like Rick Pitino play the same kind of game at Kentucky and it's called up-tempo. I guess it's in style." — Nolan Richardson (head coach at Arkansas)

Lesson 9
Trash Talk

Listen to Nick Van Exel and Reggie Miller. Call it trash talk, smack, downtalkin' or "playin' with an attitude" — it has become the norm on professional and college courts across America (and by their example, unfortunately in high school gyms and on outdoor playgrounds as well).

"Off the court, the LA's Nick Van Exel will tell you he's an all-around nice guy. Get him on the court and it's a whole different story," according to sports writer Mark Heisler. Van Exel says it's his way of motivating himself in the game. "I figure if you have an attitude on the court, it's going to make you a better player," says the Laker point guard. "I'm emotional. I like to win."

Some of his Pacer teammates and fans were concerned that Reggie Miller had lost this sort of intensity when Orlando crushed them in Game 7 of the conference play-offs in 1995. "After firing the verbal shots heard 'round Manhattan, Miller buttoned up the rest of the playoffs, and many thought the loss of swagger sapped much of his aggression," reported Dan Dunkin.

Assistant Hawk Coach Dick Helm doesn't agree that players have to be mouthy to be aggressive. He watched a change in Craig Ehlo's play that proved it. "He seems to be playing with more control, rather than in bedlam and mayhem," says Helm of Ehlo. A lot of the change is due to Ehlo's faith. "Craig has become a meeker person. The world looks at meekness as weakness," says the assistant coach, "but meekness is actually strength under control. He is a more controlled person and he plays more under control."

A pair exhibiting such control were UCLA stars Tyus Edney and Cameron Dollar. While playing together for the 1994-95 NCAA Championship Bruins, they called each other "Rated PG" — not just because both were outstanding point guards, but because they did not use foul language or indulge in the R-rated lifestyles seen in many college athletes.

"Self-control was once an admired quality among athletes we revered," says Dave Branon of *Sports Spectrum*. Legends like Oscar Robinson never uttered obscenities during a game. "It was an unspoken rule that player decorum was G-rated." Branon finds it unsettling that "While the talent is getting better, the language is getting worse." He disagrees (and rightly so) with those athletes who mistakenly think that using dirty language proves how tough you are. "The really tough athletes are the ones who can face adversity without letting fly all the profanity. It takes absolutely no self-control to use garbage language."

Branon believes some coaches are also setting poor examples — pacing and screaming their own epithets at the officials. Branon finds it refreshing, however, that there are those like former Suns' coach Paul Westphal who are able to coach and perform under control. One of the main differences in Westphal's coaching style is that he's not controlling his tongue on his own. Westphal "lives under the control of the Holy Spirit. As a believer in Jesus, Paul has the power of God's Spirit inside to help him control his emotions and his tongue."

Therein lies the power for each of us. How many times do we say things we wish we could take back? It may be cursing or profanity. It may

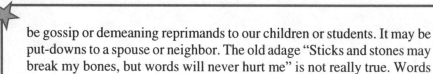

be gossip or demeaning reprimands to our children or students. It may be put-downs to a spouse or neighbor. The old adage "Sticks and stones may break my bones, but words will never hurt me" is not really true. Words do hurt.

How do you control what kind of talk comes out of your mouth?

"Do not let any unwholesome talk come out of your mouths, but only what is helpful . . . that it may benefit those who listen" (Eph. 4:29).

"I like to talk a little noise . . . but that's just on the court. I get paid to do that. It's all in the game. I don't try to get the players frustrated . . . I don't try to get them in a fighting mode. It's all about having fun." — Nick Van Exel (LA Lakers point guard)

Lesson 10

March Madness

The hype surrounding the Road to the Final Four (NCAA Championship) in March each year is second only to the frenzy of the NFL Super Bowl.

College basketball is all-consuming to many fans and analysts who make comparisons of current top squads with the dynasty teams of the past. *Athlon's 1995-96 College Preview Yearbook* ran a paper tournament of the last 32 NCAA Champions. Their Final Four teams: UCLA - 1968, UCLA - 1973, Indiana - 1976, and UNC - 1982.

The 1976 Hoosiers won Athlon's title over the 1973 Bruins. Quinn Buckner, guard on that Indiana team, said, "We were much greater as a total than we were as parts . . . all of us willingly accepted our responsibilities . . . and would come at you and change the flow of the game." Athlon's reporters said, "They are the definition of the word TEAM."

Perhaps the most interesting match-up was between UCLA 1973 and UCLA 1968. This semi-final fantasy pitted Bill Walton against Lew Alcindor (former name of Kareem Abdul-Jabbar). Coach John Wooden's teams won 10 NCAA titles in 12 years (from 1963-75) with a record of 335-12. Said former Notre Dame coach Digger Phelps: "I think Wooden could have split his teams and sent one east, and they'd still end up playing each other in the NCAA final."

The fourth Athlon pick was UNC 1982. In ESPN magazine's Top Games of the Eighties, that North Carolina team's victory over Georgetown was chosen as the best championship game of the decade. That Tarheel team (including James Worthy and Sam Perkins) beat the Hoyas 63-62 on a jump shot by freshman Michael Jordan. As of 1995, Coach Dean Smith had led teams to 21 straight NCAA appearances and has 20 or more wins for more than 25 years. Carolina has had 26 players selected in the first rounds of the NBA draft (through 1995) followed by UCLA with 25.

Many players leave school early for the NBA draft, and some college freshman have difficulty passing the ACT or SAT entrance tests now demanded under NCAA rules. Still, many NBA players took advantage of not only the basketball programs but also the academics offered at the universities.

Dikembe Mutombo graduated from Georgetown with degrees in linguistics (speaks seven languages) and diplomacy (hopes to serve on the UN Security Council someday). Others earning double degrees are: Chris Dudley — economics and political science from Yale; Bryant Smith — sociology and history from Virginia; Monty Williams — communications and theater from Notre Dame (also a 4.0 high school scholar). David Robinson scored 1320 on his SAT on entering the Naval Academy where he graduated with a degree in mathematics. Tony Bennett earned a 3.46 GPA while getting his humanistic studies degree at Wisconsin-Green Bay. Dan Schayes had a 3.5 GPA in organic chemistry from Syracuse and was a Rhodes Scholar nominee. Former NBA star and US senator Bill Bradley put off the NBA for two years after graduating from Princeton to attend Oxford (England) on his Rhodes Scholarship. More attention should be given to these scholar-athletes who set examples of gaining the knowledge and education that college offers.

Dean Smith
University of North Carolina

There is, however, a difference between knowledge and wisdom. While book knowledge is important, common sense and spiritual wisdom are even more valuable. We gain wisdom by asking God for it (James 1:5) and by studying His Word, but we also need the Holy Spirit's guidance. Bob George, in his book *Classic Christianity*, says, "I knew the Bible frontwards and backwards, but that knowledge alone didn't change my condition. In my experience, Jesus got lost in the Bible." In *The Best is Yet to Be* Leroy Patterson agrees and warns, "Sometimes we can get so caught up in the critical analysis of the text, we lose the devotional aspect." Our goal is not to have just a theological understanding of the Bible but to have a heart-to-heart relationship with Jesus Christ. That is the wisest decision of all.

"Wisdom is supreme; therefore get wisdom. Though it cost you all you have, get understanding. For wisdom will enter your heart, and knowledge will be pleasant to your soul" (Prov. 4:7, 2:10).

"It doesn't get any better than college hoops! The players, the fans, and of course, Dick Vitale!" — Robin Roberts (former college all-star, now with ESPN)

Lesson 11
Time-outs

Chris Webber will never forget the time-out he called in the final seconds of the 1993 NCAA Championship game. Unfortunately for Webber and the Wolverines, Michigan had no time-outs left and the team was charged with a technical foul. That sealed the 77-71 win for North Caroline.

Used effectively, time-outs can win (or lose a game.) Coaches call time-outs to correct problems with their team's oncourt actions and to restore order to their game plan. They also use huddle time to calm players after a questionable call by the ref or some physical altercation. Time-outs are also called to avoid time violations when in-bounding the ball or getting the ball across center court. A coach may also call for a time-out to put more pressure on an opponent who is about to shoot important free throws. These time-outs should be rare, however, because they use up the allotment of such breaks that may be crucial for instruction near the end of a close game. In these instances, the coach, clipboard in hand, diagrams the specific play he believes can score the tying or winning basket, or he may be devising key defensive strategy to keep the other team from scoring that last-second goal. Halftime offers many of the same opportunities as a time-out only with more time to rest and plan strategy. It is the time to re-group for a second effort. If your team is behind, the coach's ability to "motivate the troops" is an essential element of this locker room break. He may rant and rave to get the players to a higher level of play. Or, he may take a calm approach, using the chalkboard to make certain special plays and key strategies are fully understood by the entire team. If the team is leading, there may be a bit more levity. Boston star Larry Bird was known for his half-time pranks. One time while K.C. Jones was putting a play on the chalkboard, Bird carefully tied the coach's shoelaces together. Regardless of the atmosphere, every coach encourages the team to remain committed and play even harder in the second half.

Many of us need a similar pep talk as we near the second half of our lives. With the baby boomer generation (born from 1946 until the mid-fifties) reaching this point, counselors and psychologists are being overwhelmed with people facing the turmoil of midlife. Women have long sought help as they face the menopausal years which may produce physical and often emotional problems. Now doctors are finding that men have as difficult a time, if not worse. Thousands of men ages 35-50 end their marriages and become disenchanted with where they are in life.

Author and counselor and himself a survivor of mid-life crisis, Jim Conway offers significant suggestions for those facing this period. Get some physical exercise. It will "clear out the mind and drain off some of the emotional tension." A proper diet and getting plenty of rest is also vital. Take on new challenges (not a new family!) He suggests taking a class to broaden your interests. Take a trip. A change of scenery can provide a change of attitude. "Walking in the woods or by the ocean seemed to give me hope," says Conrad. He also found that music was significant during his crisis. While songs about young love were depressing, the wonderful lyrics and easy listening of Christian cassettes and CDs were most helpful. Spending more time in God's Word and on Christian endeavors will also help.

Share with friends, but beware that sharing emotional pain and disappointments with "just a friend" of the opposite sex is always asking for trouble. That is how intimacy begins, so find Christian friends of the same sex who care about both your emotions and spirit. Also, learn to be more open with your spouse.

Age and change do not have to be negatives. Midlife can be a time out for re-evaluation and re-commitment to our moral principles and our families. There is a Russian proverb that says: "A birthday is not a measure of how old we've become but a celebration of where we are in the magical circle of life."

Celebrate whatever your age!

"So then, banish anxiety from your heart and cast off the troubles of your body, for youth and vigor are meaningless" (Eccles. 11:10).

"I don't like all those TV time-outs. I run out of things to say to my team."
— Jim Valvano (former coach at North Carolina State)

Lesson 12
Alley-Oop

When you think about slam-dunks, who first comes to mind? Perhaps, Michael Jordan. But did you know that he did not create the "hang time from the foul line" dunk that won the 1987 All-Star Slam contest? Dr. J used that move to win the very first Slam Dunk contest in the ABA on January 27, 1976. Erving and David Thompson's competition was "one of the best sports sideshows of all time," according to Philadelphia sportswriter Jeremy Treatman. "Thompson appeared to have the contest won after a series of monster dunks, which included a 360-degree spin and a dunk in one motion, and his famed cradle, behind-the-head jam." But then Erving began walking to the other end of the court. He took off running from the opposite free throw line, and finally launched himself from the foul line. "It was incredible."

While Wilt Chamberlain, Gus Johnson, Elgin Baylor, and others were already dunking in the NBA, the creative jams of the ABA brought new excitement to the pro game. The first All-Star *NBA* Slam contest was held in 1984 with Larry Nance beating out Dr. J. Two-time slam champs are Jordan, Dominique Wilkins, and Harold Miner. Other winners include Spud Webb, Kenny Walker, Dee Brown, and Isaiah Rider. Cedric Ceballos won in 1992 with a spectacular *blindfolded* dunk he named "Hocus Pocus" in honor of Magic Johnson. Brent Barry chose the traditional foul-line soar-and-slam shot to win the contest in 1996.

University of Houston coach Guy Lewis put the dunk in the

team's play book and used it regularly during the 1983 season. Ironically, he only called for the play one time in the Final Four Championship game that they lost to NC State 54-52. How do you think the Wolfpack scored the winning basket? On a missed long shot by Derrick Wittenberg that was rebounded and slammed by Lorenzo Charles with less than one second on the game clock!

Another Charles had one of the lighter moments in jammin' history. Phoenix Suns "Sir Charles" Barkley kept getting his head in the way of his own dunks in the January 6, 1987, game against the 76ers. Officials refused to count three of Barkley's dunks because the ball bounced off his head and back out of the basket.

Another power dunker, Darryl Dawkins, became known as the "Master of Disaster" after destroying two backboards in a 22-day period. The shattering glass and delay time for a new backboard to be installed quickly brought about the development of the collapsible rim.

One of the fans' favorite dunks is the assisted "alley-oop" slam where a player like Clyde Drexler tosses a shot high toward the basket and Hakeem Olajuwon catches the ball before it reaches the rim and pounds the ball through the hoop. The "Magic Shaq and Penny Show" includes the alley-oop with O'Neal and Hardaway in Orlando. Kevin Johnson, Suns guard who offers up these mid-air assists to Barkley, says it's nothing verbal. "You just read each other naturally."

Considered the most captivating connection in the game, the success of the alley-oop depends on the catch and follow-through. That is not unlike our spiritual lives.

God's grace is freely given, but we must choose to receive it! Our parents, church school teachers, older siblings, even Christian basketball stars we admire may pass their faith along to us. We can read the Bible and other Christian books as well to gain the knowledge we need. However, until we are willing to receive Christ into our lives and follow through with a personal commitment, we will not be victorious in our spiritual lives. We can certainly learn a lot from others and should be grateful for their teaching and examples, but we must each make the decision for ourselves. Only then can we pass our faith along so others too can "catch the Spirit." Have you caught it yet?

"I pray that as you share your faith with others it will grip their lives too, as they see the wealth of good things in you that come from Christ Jesus" (Philem. 1:6;LB).

"You throw up an air ball and then Shaq goes up 15 feet to catch it and dunk it and everyone says, Wow! what a pass!" — Anfernee (Penny) Hardaway

Lesson 13
Injured

"The team picture is an x-ray," once quipped Knick publicist John Cirillo. That must have been the way coach Mike Fratello felt about the 1994-95 Cleveland Cavalier squad. Before the season even began Larry Nance had retired prematurely when his knees finally gave out after 13 years in the NBA. Brad Daughtery had undergone back surgery and Gerald Wilkins had torn his Achilles tendon. Later, Mark Price would miss eight weeks with a broken wrist, back-up point guard Terrall Brandon would miss the play-offs with a stress fracture in his right leg, and Tyrone Hill would be out for a period with hand surgery.

Price would be traded to the Washington Bullets for the next season, and then break his foot to miss at least eight weeks of another season. Couple that with Chris Webber's season-ending shoulder surgery and the team in the nation's capital was crippled early.

Being even temporarily sidelined was new to Dallas Maverick Jim Jackson. He had never missed a game due to injury in his entire career until he suffered a severe ankle sprain that put him out for the final 31 games of the 1994-95 season. "Sitting out those games was the most frustrating thing I've ever dealt with," said the former Ohio State star, "I don't want to go through that again." Said teammate Jason Kidd, "Knowing Jimmy, the injury will just motivate him to come back stronger and better."

That same comeback motivation was a factor in the rehab of Brandon University (Canada) star Tracy MacLeod. Landing awkwardly on her right leg and breaking both her tibia and fibula, she saw a nightmare unfold during the 1993 season. Circulation problems complicated her surgery and she eventually had to have her leg amputated eight inches below her knee. Who could have guessed that with a prosthesis in place, MacLeod would return at the beginning of the following season. "I wasn't about to let anyone put limitations on me," she said.

That same determination is also the story of Sacramento Kings point guard Bobby Hurley. He was nearly killed in an automobile accident on December 12 (also in 1993). He suffered a torn trachea, a torn ligament in his right knee, a fractured left shoulder, several broken ribs, and a compression fracture in his back. Hurley steadily recuperated and returned to the Kings line-up the following season.

Treating patients with severe sprains, fractures, and torn ligaments is the job of orthopedic doctor Suresh Nayak. He credits one of his mentors for teaching him the following philosophy: "I don't operate on x-rays. I operate on patients." Dr. Nayak listens and he cares.

That is the way God operates. He cares about people. It is not so much our broken bones or sins that concern Christ, but our broken spirits. He doesn't look on the outward circumstances of our lives. He sees our inner soul. Won't you let Him heal your pain — from the inside out?

Jesus answered them, "It is not the healthy who need a doctor, but the sick. I have not come to call the righteous, but sinners to repentance" (Luke 5:31-32).

"My body could stand the crutches, but my mind couldn't stand the sidelines." — Michael Jordan (while missing 64 games in 1985-86)

Fouls are a way to hold players (and coaches) accountable for their actions in a basketball game. Beyond the personal fouls on players, there are more flagrant fouls known as technicals. Using too many time-outs, failing to report a player change to the official scorekeeper, delay of game, etc., can warrant a technical. However, most "T's" are given for questioning the referee's calls or unsportsmanlike conduct — especially profanity.

The penalty for a technical includes one free throw or two (if deemed intentional or flagrant). A "T" called on the coach or another person from the bench is automatically two shots. No players line up along the lane so there are fewer distractions for the shooter. The coach chooses which player in the game shoots the basket(s) — usually the player with the best free throw percentage. This team also gets control of the ball at midcourt. If a second "T" is charged to the bench, the head coach is ejected and must leave the floor of the arena.

In addition to coach and player ejections, the NBA levies fines against the players and teams. Through mid-November of 1995, the NBA had imposed $202,500 in fines for fights and ejections since the start of the exhibition season. There were also 27 suspensions. The entire totals for the previous year had only been $143,000 and 22 suspensions. (The NCAA also doles out suspensions for extremely flagrant violations.)

Some athletes need to be suspended or held more accountable for improper conduct off the court as well. Rapes and domestic abuse are both increasing. All too often it involves athletes who have become accustomed to physical contact as acceptable behavior. Robert Parish, with third highest number of career fouls in the NBA (4,191), apparently was as aggressive at home as on the court. Charged with beating his ex-wife, Nancy Saad, Parish left an otherwise stellar basketball career under a cloud of disgrace. Although not a criminal offense, Wilt Chamberlain's bragging to the world about his "conquests with 20,000 or more women" (while traveling the country with the Knicks) was another example of an athlete being unaccountable for his sexual conduct and personal actions.

Some professional organizations and colleges try to keep these incidents of abuse or rape under wraps. Fans stick up for the athletes as if they were arrested for a speeding ticket. Coaches often reinstate players with as little as a wrist slap. No real punishment or even counseling. Not so at Indiana. After Sherron Wilkerson, a starting forward for the 1995-96 Hoosiers, left his female companion with a bleeding lip, bruised chin, and bite-marked neck, "Coach Bobby Knight wasted no time. He bounced Wilkerson from the team . . . and the school revoked the scholarship." Knight didn't offer any of the "lame excuses coaches use to cling to their hoop dreams." An editorial in *The Cincinnati Enquirer* praised Knight: "More college coaches should slam-dunk that message home."

One pro player leads the way in setting an example of personal accountability — especially in the area of sexuality and male-female relationships. Most sex education programs teach the use of condoms and "safe sex," but Phoenix Suns guard A.C. Green points another direction.

In his Athletes for Abstinence video *It Ain't Worth It*, Green hosts teenagers, medical experts, and some superstar friends (including

A.C. Green
Phoenix Suns

David Robinson) to let young people hear the message: "It is possible to wait!"

In personal appearances, Green tells young girls they do not have to give themselves to guys to prove anything. "If that is what it takes, honey, he ain't worth it!" he says in packed high school gyms. He acknowledges there are many temptations but Green shares, "I want to make a commitment to a young lady that I will cherish, value, and respect, to be her husband and her husband only." He says, "It's a matter of self-respect."

Respect and personal accountability! To oneself, to others, and to Christ!

"It is God's will that you should . . . avoid sexual immorality; that each of you should learn to control his own body in a way that is holy and honorable, not in passionate lust like the heathen" (1 Thess. 4:3-5).

"I found it to my team's advantage to not say anything to the officials. I needed to stay in the games." — Kareem Abdul-Jabbar (4,657 career fouls — highest in the NBA)

52

Lesson 15
Million Dollar Contracts

Do you know what the word Nike means? It's Greek in origin and means "victory." To many young players today, victory and success are too tied up in the marketplace and ads like Nike and others. "Sport, to these kids, is just another form of entertainment," says Chicago Bulls coach Phil Jackson. "They're paid performers and what they want is a commercial to establish them as unique persons."

That doesn't mean we scorn every player with a soda or shoe ad. After all, the NBA itself runs commercials. The "I love this game" ads are representative of what Commissioner David Stern sees as a part of making the league "a global provider of entertainment, whether it's programming or licensed products." (Advertising Age)

Popular stars like Michael Jordan and Shaquille O'Neal are seen on everything from paper plates, greeting cards, and gift wrap to soft drinks, fast food, and shoe ads. Several players have lucrative off-the-court contracts including Grant Hill, who plays the piano in one ESPN promo, and Penny Hardaway. His multi-million-dollar deal with Nike and the clever Li'l Penny ads with the animated doll in his own goateed likeness have become fan favorites.

Still everyone else is second to Jordan, who has appeared on more individual Wheaties packages (14 to date) than any other sports celebrity. Patti Jo Sinopoli, with Quaker Oats Co. (parent company of Gatorade), says "it would take a psychologist to explain how Michael Jordan's charm and charisma work." The only person to endorse the sports drink in its 30-year history, Jordan's year-and-a-half retirement while he tried major league baseball had no impact on sales. "When we signed him for 10 years, we knew he would retire before the contract ran out. But with Michael's popularity, it didn't matter." Jordan defines what an athlete spokesperson is.

Women are finally getting their chance at basketball promotions as well. Sheryl Swoopes is the first female to have a shoe named after her (by Nike). Rebecca Lobo also has a shoe endorsement for Reebok plus other deals with Spalding and a Connecticut-based Chevrolet dealer.

Players and coaches make money endorsing businesses and products on local television and radio. College mentors John Thompson, Bobby Knight, and Rick Pitino all starred together in a national commercial for Taco Bell. If you look closely at many coaches attire during a game, you will notice little Nike or Reebok pins on their lapels. These coaches and players also support many worthwhile programs and charities both locally and nationwide.

As a part of David Robinson's million-dollar deal with Nike, he convinced the company to sponsor a "Stay-in-School" program. For any company that gets Robinson's endorsement, they have to agree to help children in some way. While we don't read about it in the magazines or newspapers, most basketball stars are not greedy but share their wealth.

How well do we share our wealth? Having smaller salaries does not immune us from greed. It doesn't have so much to do with an amount as it does an attitude. Richard Foster talks about the "misery" that accompanies "restless gnawing greed." He says, "We plunge ourselves into enormous debt and then take two and three jobs to stay afloat. We uproot our families with unnecessary moves just so we can have a more prestigious house. We grasp and grasp and never have enough."

When Jesus told the rich young man that it would be harder for a camel to go through the eye of a needle than for a rich man to enter the kingdom of God, He was not saying that persons of wealth would be excluded from heaven. He was saying to all of us that whatever we put ahead of Him — whatever it is that we want more of than we want of His teachings and His way of life — that is what we worship. That is what will keep us from fully serving Him. A sign on a church bulletin board questioned: Do you use people to gain more money, or do you use money to help more people?

"Whoever loves money never has money enough; whoever loves wealth is never satisfied with his income" (Eccles. 5:10).

"For me, the key is learning to draw the line between possessing things and things possessing me. The more you're exposed to, the more you want. It's a challenge to draw the line between spoiling yourself and recognizing that the Lord is blessing you." — David Robinson (San Antonio Spurs)

Lesson 16
Dynamic Duos

"From the early years to today, great 1-2 punches have packed a real wallop in quest for the NBA crown." That was the sub-title for the Sporting News 1995-96 Yearbook article, "Thanks for the Complement." Sportswriter David Moore put together an extensive list of successful NBA duos.

Kareem Abdul-Jabbar and Magic Johnson led the Lakers to five championships. When asked what he learned from Jabbar during his rookie season, Johnson replied, "Give him the ball!" In his early career Jabbar also teamed with the great Oscar Robertson to win a title for the Milwaukee Bucks. While Robertson and Jerry Lucas never won rings for the Cincinnati Royals, they did share 13 All Star games and 1960 Olympic Gold Medals. Jerry West and Elgin Baylor never won an NBA crown while playing together for the Lakers, but both averaged over 27 points for their career and led the team to seven finals. Willis Reed and Dave DeBusschere led the Knicks to two NBA titles. The 76ers saw more than one dynamic tandem: Wilt Chamberlain and Hal Greer in the 1960s and Julius Erving and Moses Malone in the 1980s. Famous Celtic pairs include Bill Russell and Bob Cousy (11 NBA titles) and Larry Bird and Kevin McHale (3 championships).

Modern day double-stars go to Bulls Michael Jordan and Scottie Pippen — need we say more than "Three-peat!" With the all-time assist leader John Stockton at his side, Karl Malone has enjoyed ten years with the Jazz. "It's like a dream," said Clyde Drexler when the Rockets made the trade that re-matched him with former (Houston) college teammate Hakeem Olajuwon. Rising on the horizon are Reggie Miller and Rick Smits (Pacers), Shawn Kemp and Gary Payton (Supersonics), Glenn Robinson and Vin Baker (Bucks), and Chris Webber and Juwan Howard (Bullets).

Dubbed "Orlando's Whiz Kids," Shaquille O'Neal and Penny Hardaway are written about as "a pair of precocious 23-year-old stars" to whom the future belongs. Even Drexler, whose Rocket team defeated them in the 1995 NBA Championship, says, "With those two as the cornerstones, I wouldn't be surprised to see that team in the Finals every year throughout the rest of this decade." The only thing that may eventually stop them is a difference in goals. "Hardaway burns to be a champion. He also yearns to be not just a great player, but the very best in the game," reports Lyle Spencer, a Riverside (CA) columnist. On the other hand, O'Neal has too many irons in the fire. Shaq's look on the future, "I want to win one or two [titles] and retire with time to do something else around 29 or 30." However long Shaq sticks around and they continue to complement one another, there's no stopping them.

Check the "e" in complement. It doesn't mean doling out praise to one another. Complement means to make complete or whole, to bring to perfection. Nowhere else should this be better seen than with a husband and wife. God created woman to make man complete, to be a suitable helper for him (Gen. 2: 20-23). A married couple should be more than just the sum of the two persons. They create for one another an intellectual, emotional, and spiritual climate where each can grow and become far more than either could have ever been alone.

This takes more than mere feelings. It takes commitment. While divorce rates continue to climb, "family values" have become the "in" political agenda. But we can't wait for politicians or other leaders to find ways to put marriages and family life back together. If we will each commit to our own spouses and families, we can become the building blocks that put politics and government back together.

In his 1995 visit to the United States, Pope John Paul II implored people to recommit themselves as spouses and parents. The pontiff said, "There can be no life worthy of the human person without a culture — and a legal system — that honors and defends marriage and the family."

"A man will leave his father and mother and be united to his wife" (Gen. 2:24).

"What God has joined together, let man not separate" (Mark 10:9).

"You find yourself choosing your own poison. Do you double Shaq or Penny? Do you try to take away Shaq's dunk and give Penny the outside shot? It's enough to make you pull your hair out." — Dennis Johnson (assistant coach and former player for the Celtics)

Lesson 17
Rejection

Hall of Famer (1983) John Havlicek played college basketball at Ohio State with Bobby Knight. Says Havlicek of the Indiana coach, "It's strange, Bobby was the worst defensive player on the team, yet his teams now are so defense oriented." Knight obviously learned the essentials whether he played them well himself or not. While the main objective of basketball is to "get the ball through the hoop" more often than your opponent, another theory is to stop the other guys from scoring. That translates to "a strong defense is often the best offense"— a game plan of many successful coaches including Knight, Dean Smith at UNC, and John Thompson at Georgetown.

There are many elements of a strong defense — being aggressive on the backboards, various zone attacks on your opponent's end of the court, the full-court press, trapping (two-on-one defense of the ball handler) and intense individual play.

Coach and author Larry Jones shares advice on how to steal the ball. His mentor and former coach Abe Lemon used K.C. Jones (who was playing for the Celtics at that time) as an example. "He always comes up on the ball. That makes it easier to get, and if you accidentally hit your opponent's hand, it doesn't make as much noise," taught Lemon. It also "lessens the chances of your getting a foul."

The player to watch today is Utah's John Stockton. This all-time NBA leader in assists now claims the top spot in steals as well. In February 1996

(Jazz against the Celtics) Stockton overtook Maurice Cheeks, who had 2,130 career steals in 15 seasons with the 76ers. Stockton broke the record in his 12th season. A prolonged ovation halted the game temporarily as Stockton was presented with flowers, a plaque. and the game ball. Not one to enjoy such hoopla, Stockton said he was glad when it was over.

Other top NBA players to watch in their ball thievery are Scottie Pippen, Mookie Blaylock, Gary Payton, Jason Kidd, Nate McMillan, Eddie Jones, and Penny Hardaway. Not surprisingly, it is the taller players to watch in another defensive category — blocked shots. Retired Laker Kareem Abdul-Jabbar leads in career blocks or rejections with 3,189. Not far behind is retired Jazz Mark Eaton with 3,064. The current player on track to break the record is Hakeem Olajuwon who had 2,983 at the end of the 1994-95 season. However, Dikembe Mutombo has out-rejected Hakeem in recent seasons, averaging almost 4 blocks per game and over 300 per season. Other NBA leaders are Shawn Bradley, Alonzo Mourning, Shaquille O'Neal, and David Robinson (who holds NCAA records in rejections: 516 career, 207 season and 14 in one game).

While a rejection is to be cheered on the basketball court, it is a devastating emotional feeling in one's personal life. Nobody likes to be turned down when you ask for a date or apply for a job (or send a query for a book idea). It hurts one's self-esteem. But we must realize that rejection is a part of life. In Minirth-Meier's *Complete Life Encyclopedia* they offer this healthy advice: "Don't take it personally. Don't take rejection as a sign that you are 'no good.' If you don't get this job (or date or offer), you'll get another. Don't let rejection stop you from going out and trying again." They also suggest that rejections may be a

David Robinson
San Antonio Spurs

way for us to re-evaluate and move in new directions.

The most painful rejections we face are from loved ones. Many patients in mental wards or suffering depression have begun their downward spirals at the hands of unloving parents. If this is your case, seek out support and counseling. If you are a parent, make encouraging your children and accepting them for who they are (not what you may want them to be) your top priority.

There is One who will always love us just as we are. He never rejects us. He loves us even when we are unlovable and sinners. No matter how often you may have been rejected by others, Jesus Christ offers acceptance and forgiveness that will surround you with inner peace and love.

"Praise be to God, who has not rejected my prayer or withheld his love from me!" (Ps. 66:20).

"It was distracting with what was going on inside myself . . . second-guessing myself if I reached for a ball and my guy would score . . . not taking foolish chances to hurt your team." — John Stockton (2/20/96 after steal-record-breaking game)

Lesson 18
Ball Hog or Hot Dog

The term "ball hog" is self-descriptive. This "Me, Me, Me!" show-off with the "hot dog" attitude shoots whenever he gets the ball, even if it's not an open shot. He enjoys being the center of attention. Ball hogs or hot dogs often score a lot of points, but that doesn't always translate into a team's success.

While Wilt Chamberlain was not a selfish player (he often led his team in assists), he certainly shot the ball more than anyone on the court. In one high school game he scored 90 points — 60 coming in one 12-minute period. No one else would have had time to get their hands on the ball! At the University of Kansas he set school scoring records, but there were no national championships for the Jayhawks during his tenure. His NBA records stand alone making him one of the best ever, and yet in his 14-year career, he led his teams to only 2 NBA titles. On March 2, 1962, Wilt scored 100 points in the Warriors' 169-147 win over the Knicks. (Was any defense played in the game?!) In the latter days of his career, coaches requested Wilt "shoot less" so they could "try to win more." During the final five years of his career Wilt's scoring average dropped, but he helped the Lakers to the NBA Finals four times.

Perhaps the best known hot dog of his time was Pete Maravich. Called Pistol Pete (for "pulling the trigger" or unleashing the ball from anywhere on the court), Maravich held nearly every NCAA scoring record: career points (3,667), highest career average (44.2), most field goal attempts

(3,166) and made (1,387), and most career 50-point games (28). Considered the greatest basketball player in LSU history, the teams' combined record during his seasons: 49-35. His NBA years were no less "showmanship" but equally unsuccessful in terms of team victories. With the Atlanta Hawks and the New Orleans-turned-Utah Jazz, Pete continued his "playground moves, circus shots and hot dog passes" (considered "outrageous during his era" according to Microsoft's Complete NBA Basketball). Often leading the team in rebounds, steals, and assists, he was not always selfish, but his flamboyance certainly provided a "one man show." Named to the Hall of Fame in 1986, Maravich died two years later at the age of 40 from a heart attack suffered while playing three-on-three with *Focus on the Family's* Jim Dobson and other close friends.

Modern hot dog, Pacers Reggie Miller, can take control of a game and dominate the opponent not only with his scoring, but with his attitude. It's not a "hit 'em and hustle nonchalantly down the court" like Michael Jordan. Miller "hits 'em and sticks it in your face." In the fourth quarter of one 1994 play-off game in New York, Reggie scored 25 points and let courtside Knick fan and entertainer Spike Lee know it. Miller became an instant media hit — appearing on *Letterman*, *Leno*, and *Regis & Kathie Lee*. He put on a similar one man show in the 1995 play-offs against Atlanta, with 29 points in the first half. While Miller does not avoid the limelight, neither does he crave it. Sportswriter Tim Sullivan reported, "If Miller was guilty of anything this season, it was selflessness. He averaged 19.6 points and took 502 fewer shots than Shaquille O'Neal." Reggie himself said, "Don't look for me to be the next Michael Jordan. I don't want to score that many points. That would be taking away from our team." Yet Sullivan charges, [Miller] "can no longer be that generous. The Pacers . . . will need maximum Miller if they are to proceed." Sullivan believes Reggie needs to be more of a ball hog.

In our Christian lives, however, being a "hot dog for the Lord" somehow does not sound very sincere. "An isolated Christian is a paralyzed Christian!" was one message on an Emmaus retreat weekend. Another retreat leader warned, "God doesn't need any Lone Ranger Christians." (Even the Lone Ranger had Tonto!) We need to be careful that we don't get so caught up in our own game plan for God that we forget to seek His direction. Local pastor (and a chaplain for the 1996 US Olympic teams) Brad Olson reminds us, "We can get so caught up in the work of the Lord that we forget the Lord of the work."

"For everyone who exalts himself will be humbled, and he who humbles himself will be exalted" (Luke 18:14).

"If I want to watch great individuals play, I'll watch golf or track." — John Wooden (all-time winning coach at UCLA, Hall of Fame 1972)

Lesson 19
From the Charity Line

NCAA rules prohibit official basketball team practices until October 15. In 1970 Maryland coach Lefty Driesell told the media he was so excited that he couldn't wait any longer so he scheduled a 12:01 a.m. practice. Now televised by ESPN with basketball guru Dick Vitale as host, today's version takes place on many premier college campuses as "Midnight Madness." While all the fanfare provides excitement and promotes college basketball, the kickoff represents the core of every team's success — practice.

NBA Hall of Famer (1982) Bill Bradley lived by the "practice" motto of many coaches: "Teams are made during the season, players during the off-season." While in high school, Bradley worked for a summer on Capitol Hill. Each evening he would stop by a local gym, mark 6 or 8 spots on the court and practice until he made 50 baskets from each spot. (That summer may have been instrumental in both his NBA and US Senate careers.)

One area where individual commitment can pay off is from the free-throw line. Why should coaches waste minutes of team practice when players can practice foul shots on their own? And some players obviously need the practice!

"Brick shots" (misses) from the line were significant in the closing minutes of several 1995 NBA play-off games. Round 2, Game 1, Knicks vs. Pacers, score tied: John Starks missed two free throws.

Round 2, Game 1, Orlando up by two: Michael Jordan missed two. Round 2, Game 2, Lakers-Spurs, score tied: Vlade Divac missed two. Round 2, Game 5: Suns Charles Barkley missed two against Houston. Houston would benefit again in their 120-118 win in Game 1 of the Finals when Orlando's Nick Anderson missed four consecutive free throws in the last 10 seconds of the game. In 1990 Nets center Clevis Dudley missed 17 of 18 from the line — 13 in a row in the final quarter — in the 124-113 loss to the Pacers.

Wilt Chamberlain was so bad from the stripe (52 percent career FTs) that the Celtics once hired Cy Kaselman (95 percent shooter one year) to work with Wilt in the off-season. He improved to nearly 70 percent, but refused to continue because he "felt like a sissy" shooting the underhand style taught by Kaselman.

That two-handed underhand shot was the trademark of Rick Barry, the only player yet to retire with a 90 percent career FT average. The NBA average is 72 percent. Players with the best career average (to date) include Mark Price (91 percent), Rick Barry, Calvin Murphy, Scott Skiles, and Larry Bird. Today's leading foul shooters, along with Price and Skiles, are Spud Webb, Dana Barros, Reggie Miller, Muggsy Bogues, Mahmoud Abdul-Rauf, and B.J. Armstrong.

To improve free-throw percentage, practice is the key. Establish a routine. Always hold the ball the same way, bounce it the same number of times, focus on a specific spot, breathe the same way, etc. Visualize as you fall asleep. See yourself making 10, 20, 50 in a row. Marquette Professor of Psychology Anees Sheikh says, "Research shows mental practice can have the same effect as real practice . . . you are creating a model of

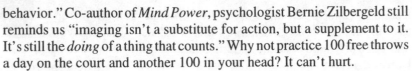

behavior." Co-author of *Mind Power*, psychologist Bernie Zilbergeld still reminds us "imaging isn't a substitute for action, but a supplement to it. It's still the *doing* of a thing that counts." Why not practice 100 free throws a day on the court and another 100 in your head? It can't hurt.

Combining physical and mental practices in our spiritual life can't hurt either. What is your devotional routine? God tells us to think about His commands at four specific times during the day: *"when you sit at home and when you walk along the road, when you lie down and when you get up"* (Deut. 6:7). Putting these into modern routines, consider these study or practice times: (1) during bathroom breaks (keep devotionals or a small Bible in what we jokingly call "the library"); (2) driving to work, school, meetings, or practice (nobody walks; use traffic jam time to listen to Christian radio); (3) when you can't sleep (prayer and Bible memory can make even insomnia useful); and (4) in the morning shower (why not sing a favorite hymn?)

In both our devotions and basketball, the key is practice, practice, practice.

"Whoever practices and teaches these commands will be called great in the kingdom of heaven" (Matt. 5:19).

"Basketball camps are great but going to camp won't improve your scoring. You have to practice what you learn! Practice by doing, do by practicing." — Glenn "Doc" Rivers (Hawks, Clippers, Knicks, Spurs, through 1996)

Lesson 20
Worldwide Net

Basketball has become the most popular sport in the world. In 1987 FIBA (the Federation de Basketball International) and the NBA finally reached terms regarding amateur versus professional play. That same year McDonald's began sponsoring a round robin tournament between a premier NBA squad and top Europeans. The Milwaukee Bucks played in the inaugural event against teams from the Soviet Union and Italy. Other NBA teams have been Celts to Madrid in 1988; Nuggets - Rome, 1989; Knicks - Barcelona, 1990; Lakers - Paris, 1991; (Olympics in 1992); and Suns - Munich, 1993. The McDonald's tournament now features six top global teams with the US sending the NBA Champs.

The 1992 Summer Olympics in Barcelona, Spain, spurred even more international interest as Dream Team I composed of top US professionals (and lone collegiate Christian Laettner) won the Gold Medal by an average margin of 44 points. With Michael Jordan, Magic Johnson, Charles Barkley, John Stockton, Karl Malone, Patrick Ewing, John Stockton, Scottie Pippen, David Robinson, Chris Mullen, Clyde Drexler, and Larry Bird, it's no surprise that these Olympic Games caused an explosion of interest in the NBA abroad. Dream Team II played in the 1994 Pan Am Games with several of the '92 stars. Dream Team III, with dynamic additions like Grant Hill, Shaquille O'Neal, and Reggie Miller will represent the US at the 1996 Olympics in Atlanta. The only player on three Olympic teams ('88, '92, '96), David Robinson was especially gratified with the 1992 Gold Medal victory. The 1988 US team had been upset and settled for the bronze medal behind the USSR and Yugoslavia.

Toni Kukoc was a member of that 1988 Yugoslavia Gold Medal team (and a member of the Croatian team in 1992). He would then come to the US to play alongside Jordan and Pippen for the Chicago Bulls. Foreign players today are making an immediate impact upon their arrival on the NBA scene. In addition to Kukoc, foreign players include Dino Radja (Croatia); Sarunas Marciuluinis and Arvidas Sabonis (Lithuania); Vlade Divac (Serbia), Patrick Ewing (Jamaica), Rik Smits (Holland), Detlef Schrempf (Germany), Dikembe Mutombo (Zaire), Luc Longley (Australia), Manute Bol (Sudan), Carl Herrera (Venezuela), and Gheorghe Muresan (Romania). Hakeem Olajuwon was born in Nigeria, played college hoops at Houston, and became an American citizen in 1993.

NBA teams now play pre-season games in Mexico, Japan, and Russia. By 1996 NBA games were being televised in 170 countries around the globe with more foreign broadcasters appearing courtside every day. "NBA Fastbreak" is the Japanese broadcast hosted by Yuichi Tabata. RAFAGA-NBA is the Mexican equivalent co-hosted by Alex Blanco and Marken Mata. With new franchise teams in Toronto and Vancouver, and Commissioner David Stern considering Mexico for a possible expansion team in the near future, the NBA is truly becoming international.

We need to expand our interests to a more global level as well. We can be involved through individual support of missionary projects or through our denominational missions programs.

An interdenominational organization out of Greenwood, Indiana, OMS has a more modern approach to winning souls for Christ in the Philippines. Rather than starting in the poverty-stricken areas of Manila, Rev. and Mrs. Bill Oden established ties in the middle and upper classes. When they first arrived in 1983 Joyce Oden began teaching fashion color coordination to the wives of US diplomats and their Filipino counterparts. Mixing the program with biblical verses and principles, Joyce was able to invite some of these ladies into her home for Bible study. From these home studies, God's work has grown into Faith Evangelical Fellowship, the home church that supports numerous planted churches and Faith Bible College. Filipinos are now becoming pastors, pastors' wives, Christian educators, and leaders. By beginning with the middle class, these leaders will someday be able to help make the church in the Philippines self-sufficient. Faith is now also sending missionaries to other countries — reaching out around the world.

We too must reach out in some way to help others around the world come to know Christ. What can you do? Where can you go? Whom can you support? For whom are you praying?

"Therefore, go and make disciples of all nations, baptizing them in the name of the Father and of the Son and of the Holy Spirit" (Matt. 28:19).

"To participate in an international event with my team and as an American, that is something very important to me." — Hakeem Olajuwon (on his selection to Dream Team III)

Lesson 21
"That's the Way the Ball Bounces!"

Life isn't always fair! A perfectly executed shot bounces off the rim. A pass takes a bad bounce into an opponent's hands. A "heave-and-hope-shot" from 3/4 court banks off the backboard and through the net to win the game for the other team. Players and fans go away shaking their heads, saying "WOW!" if they won, or "Why?" if they lost.

Why? At age 24, Maurice Stokes was on his way to a stellar pro career. Named the NBA Rookie-of-the-Year with the Cincinnati Royals, he became one of the most consistent well-rounded players in the game. By the end of his third season, he averaged 16 points, 17 rebounds, and 5 assists per game. In the final season game, Stokes fell on his head while hustling for a rebound. He was briefly knocked unconscious but was able to re-enter the game.

He played in the opening post-season game in Detroit and had 12 points and 15 rebounds. On the flight back to Cincinnati, the "ball took a horrendous bounce." Stokes went into a massive seizure and fell unconscious. Rushed to the hospital, he was given the last rites of the Roman Catholic Church. He lay in a coma for six months. Doctors decided the earlier fall had caused swelling in the brain developing post-traumatic encephalopathy. At his bedside, his mother knew their steelworking family from Pittsburgh did not have the finances to care for their son.

Royal teammate Jack Twyman promised that he would take care of it. He filed with the court to become Stokes' legal guardian, was able to get workman's compensation for him, and convinced the NBA to stage a benefit exhibition game. Contributions poured in from across the nation.

Twyman provided more than legal and financial assistance. He visited Stokes almost daily. Maury regained consciousness with his mental capabilities intact and eventually recovered limited use of some of his muscles (enough he could sculpt and paint with tools strapped to his hand). He wrote on a special typewriter and could make basic sounds. Twyman took him for rides in his wheelchair, and they received a standing ovation at a basketball fund raising game. A little over a year into his retirement (after 11 NBA seasons), Twyman would bury his friend and former teammate. Vulnerable to infection, Stokes died of pneumonia.

When asked WHY he had been so devoted to Stokes, Twyman simply responded, "Why not?" That is the question we all need to learn. This healthier question moves us along to the even better question of "What now?"

That was the attitude of North Caroline State's head coach Jim Valvano, who battled cancer so valiantly. His passion for life motivated him to believe that "Anything can happen!" Accepting the 1993 Arthur Ashe ESPY Award (for courage) less than a year before his death, Valvano shared his philosophy: "If you never stop believing in and loving each other, you can accomplish miracles." Valvano lives on today through "The V Foundation" — a charitable organization started in large part by ESPN and his courtside friend Dick Vitale. The foundation is dedicated to research, advocacy, education, and fund raising toward a cure for cancer. Valvano's favorite saying became the motto for the foundation: "Don't give up, Don't ever give up!" Valvano refused to question, "Why?"

Why do innocent children suffer, often at the hands of loved ones? Why can't some caring couples have a baby? Why does a loving God allow such cruelty in the world? We've all asked these and similar questions.

Nearing the end of his own lengthy battle with cancer, Christian author and speaker Bob Benson found an answer. In the final days of his life, Bob was barely able to speak. One morning his wife, Peggy, asked, "Bob, you talk with God a lot. Have you ever asked Him why this is happening to us?" In that quiet little voice that had always been his trademark, Bob mustered a faint smile and nodded, "Yes. He said when we get to the place where we know the answers, the questions won't matter any more."

"We can see and understand only a little about God now . . . but someday we are going to see him in his completeness. . . . Now all that I know is hazy and blurred, but then I will see everything clearly" (1 Cor. 13:12;LB).

"First of all, pray to God. Don't stop living. Enjoy life. No matter what happens . . . if you're handicapped, HIV positive, whatever it is . . . put that smile on your face and continue to live." — Magic Johnson (1/30/96 in courtside TNT interview on his return after 3 years away from the Lakers due to testing HIV positive)

Lesson 22

Feminine Clipboards and Microphones

Imagine the thrill of interviewing your own brother on national television! Three-time college player-of-the-year at USC and a gold medalist in 1984, Cheryl Miller did just that with her brother Reggie at the 1996 All-Star festivities. One of the premier commentators for both women's and men's games, Cheryl teased, "I was able to beat Reggie until he started dunkin' on me." Before turning to broadcasting, she also coached at her alma mater. The only female coach inducted into the Hall of Fame (to date) is Margaret Wade (1984). Her combined high school and college record was 610-112. Each year the Wade Trophy is now awarded to a top female player.

One of today's top coaches is Tara VanDerveer. Her 10 years at Stanford earned an impressive winning percentage of over .800, and three PAC-10 and National Coach-of-the-Year awards. A 3-year starter and dean's list scholar at Indiana University (1975), she also had a 110-37 record in five years at Ohio State, was twice the Big Ten Coach-of-the-Year. Currently on leave from Stanford, VanDerveer is head coach of the USA Women's National Team that will compete in the 1996 Olympics in Atlanta. Assisting her will be Kansas coach Marian Washington, a member of the 1984 and 1988 US Olympic teams. Head coaches Ceal Barry (Colorado) and Nancy Darsch (Ohio

State) are the other 1996 Olympic assistants.

Two other successful female coaches are Jody Conradt (Texas) with over 600 career wins, and Pat Summitt (Tennessee) with 578-132 at the end of the 1994-95 season. Another ground breaker is Kerri McTiernan, the first female head coach of a men's collegiate program. According to an ESPN report she conducted tryouts at Kingsborough Community College in part with some one-on-one play. "No one she beat made the team."

ESPN has been a leader in promoting women in broadcasting. Like Cheryl Miller, another former college all-star-turned-broadcaster, Robin Roberts co-anchors ESPN Sportcenter. Both Roberts and Suzy Kolber (ESPN/ESPN2 anchor) cover all kinds of sports. ESPN Radio hired the first women to host a national radio sports talk show. Nanci Donnellan, better known as the Fabulous Sports Babe, is knowledgeable on nearly any sport you can name, admits when she isn't, and "absolutely!" loves to play the game of golf. The Babe has an easy acceptance of who she is and doesn't compete with her male counterparts. She is just "the Babe" and as such the guys have accepted her as well.

Being comfortable with ourselves and accepting one another — our differences and our sameness — is a key in any male-female relationship. Explaining these premises put *Men Are from Mars, Women are from Venus* on the best seller list. In *Hidden Keys to Loving Relationships,* Gary Smalley brings a more Christian approach to understanding these basic differences in order to diffuse hostility and create a more caring atmosphere in our homes. One of his best (and more humorous) explanations deals with our method of shopping. He calls it "Bagging the

Blouse." A man will walk into a store, ask if they have a white, long-sleeve, button-down shirt. If not, he's "out of there" and on to the next store. Within 15 minutes he can usually make the purchase. However, the wife goes to the first store and looks at all of the blouses — regardless of color, collar, or style. She may also check out the skirts, pajamas, and perfume. Even if she finds the exact blouse at the first store, she has to make certain "another store doesn't have it for a better price." Neither method is right or wrong; neither is better.

Yet we let our different approaches start all sorts of battles from shopping warfare to disciplining the kids to where to vacation. Why must it always be a competition? The more we learn to accept one another's differences instead of getting into verbal (or worse) fights, the happier we will all be. After all, God did not make us all the same. He had His reasons. Maybe it's time we try to understand and appreciate them — and each other.

"So God created man in his own image . . . male and female created he them" (Gen. 1:27).

"Overcoming my sister's shadow has been one of the biggest challenges of my career." — Reggie Miller (Indiana Pacers)

Lesson 23
Whistle-blowers

In a highly unusual display of vehemence on his part, Clyde Drexler was ejected from one of the 1995 play-off games between Houston and Phoenix. Suns Charles Barkley commented on it in a post-game interview: "I was surprised. Clyde just can't put himself in that situation, especially with Jake [O'Donnell], Mike Matthis, Steve Jaffe, and Jerry Carlton. They'll toss you . . . in a heartbeat."

Twenty-eight-year veteran referee (and now supervisor) Norm Drucker confirms Barkley's amazement, "Usually the superstars have very little to say to the officials. They play and are not distracted, no matter what the call may be." Still, according to one *Inside the NBA* analyst, "Sometimes there are things that go on that you don't know — like maybe a player has a history with a certain official. And sometimes an official will say something to a player that you can't say to him." But a player doesn't have a whistle so he must keep things in proper perspective.

Grant Hill of the Detroit Pistons shares the best perspective, "As a rookie you get a lot of calls you think are bad. But I've always tried to show respect to the officials."

Fans are another story. They seem to lack respect for the officials. Drucker says, "Fan are not objective, and in their efforts to motivate their team they see the officials as the enemy."

At one time, fans actually came to watch the refs — at least old-timer Matthew "Pat" Kennedy, who was known for his shrill whistle, finger-wagging style, and resonant voice. His style didn't always sit well, but he was the first referee voted into the Naismith Hall of Fame.

Do refs ever give "make up" calls? Drucker says, "I'd like to think 99 percent were good calls, but some are real clinkers. Most in the basketball family understand that you don't compound it by making another error."

These traits should apply to all of us in every walk of life. In *Little Lamb, Who Made Thee,* Valparaiso University professor Walter Wangerin Jr. writes: "The Law of Fairness . . . maintains a structure that all can understand. . . . In any game, it's good that there are rules, and good to know the rules, and good that referees are watching the rules. Each individual may now play heartily, and the winner is a winner after all." Wangerin goes on to remind us that as we teach "The Law of Fairness" to our children (and we must!) we must also teach that life won't always be fair. The best team doesn't always win. In doing our best, someone else may be even better. However, without some benchmark for good and evil, we would have total lawlessness and chaos. Jesus said, *"Do not think I have come to abolish the Law or the Prophets; I have not come to abolish them but to fulfill them"* (Matt. 5:17). Following the rules is one way to achieve at least a level of fairness, and God's laws are the most important to follow.

"I desire to do your will, O my God; your law is within my heart" (Ps. 40:8).

"Officiating is the only occupation in the world where the highest accolade is silence." — Earl Strom (NBA referee)

Lesson 24
Call Me Coach!

Coaches are certainly one of the most important factors in the success of any team. Lenny Wilkens became the all-time winning coach in the NBA on 1/6/95, surpassing Red Auerbach's 938 victories. In March of 1996, Wilkens (coaching the Hawks) went on to become the only NBA coach with 1,000 wins. Former Celtic Hall of Famer (1968), Auerbach says of coaching: "The secret in managing people is knowing what each person needs. People need to be free to perform."

Successful at UNLV for many years, Jerry Tarkanian (a.k.a. "The Shark") didn't find enough freedom for himself in the NBA. His pro coaching career began and ended with the Spurs after only 20 games. Winning 5 out of the first 7 games, but then losing 9 of the next 13, Tark wasn't used to 11 losses in 2-3 whole seasons at UNLV.

North Carolina's Dean Smith doesn't care to even try the "win at all cost" pressure of pro basketball. "If you make every game a life-and-death thing, you're going to have problems," says the coaching icon. "You'll be dead a lot!" Smith hasn't had that problem at UNC. His worst record in over 25 years is 21-13! Rick Pitino chose the college ranks over his coaching days in the pros. The Kentucky leader jokes, "It gives you a nice warm feeling to know you're the highest paid guy in the huddle."

Successful Arkansas coach Nolan Richardson would listen to offers from the NBA because of the money, but he doesn't want to handle the egos of professional players.

College coaching great himself, John Wooden (UCLA) and Red Auerbach were guest speakers at the 1995 Legends of High School Basketball banquet. The four coaches honored were: Bill Krueger (1075-248), Robert Hughes (1073-184), Morgan Wooten (1071-159), and Ralph Tasker (1067-275). "We've seen it all," says Krueger. "The long hair and the short. The Chuck Taylors [those are old sneakers, for you young folks!] and now these shoes that cost 150 bucks." They all began their careers in the simplistic era of Norman Rockwell and continue to coach while spectators must pass through a metal detector.

Metal detectors are nothing new for another coach of 14-18 year olds. Carolyn Malone is the only female basketball coach in the Bronx Police Athletic League in New York City. Honorable Mention winner in *USA Weekend's* Most Caring Coaches Awards, Malone has taken "kids who are on their way to [juvenile] hall and given them something to build a life around."

From after-school programs to high school and college gyms around the country in both men's and women's programs, other female coaches have made their mark. All of them, like Malone, have earned the respect and trust of their teams.

"Respect and trust" are the two things a coach must have, according to "Doc" Rivers who has played in the NBA for Mike Fratello, Larry Brown, Pat Riley, and Bob Hill. "If they [the players] trust you, they will follow you," he says. "By trust, I mean players must believe you [as the coach] are committed to the things you say."

The word commitment sums up a coach's lifestyle and goes beyond the court. Coach Mike Krzyzewski, who led Duke University to 4 Final

John Wooden
In his playing days at Purdue

Fours in a row (losing 1989 and 1990; winning 1991 and 1992), keeps in touch with his players long after they leave campus. When an automobile accident in Sacramento almost took Bobby Hurley's life, Coach K flew to the former Duke star's bedside. "I'm never too busy to talk with any of those guys," says Coach K. "A player-coach relationship ought to last a lifetime."

Commitment is important in all our relationships. "Being there no matter what!" provides the security we each need for joy and peace. Who has always been there for you? To whom are you fully committed? God has always been committed to us. He is faithful and steadfast.

Lloyd John Ogilvie, says, "Our faithfulness is not our human follow-through, but our trust that Christ will follow through in all of life's changes and challenges. He says, 'You can depend on me!' Can we say that to Him and to others? His dependability makes us dependable."

"For great is his love toward us, and the faithfulness of the Lord endures forever" (Ps. 117:2).

[about the 1995 Bruin team]: "Even though I've played in the NBA, experiencing victory as a coach for the national championship team with these guys has been my greatest thrill in sports." — Lorenzo Romar (UCLA Assistant Coach, formerly with the NBA Warriors, Bucks, and Pistons, and former player-coach for Athletes in Action)

Lesson 25
The Final Buzzer

In the semi-final game of the 1973 conference play-offs the Bulls were one point down and in possession of the ball. Somehow oblivious to the shot clock, they let the time run out. Said coach Dick Motta afterwards, "It would have been a better loss to have missed the shot. But to have not even taken a shot. . . ." He couldn't even finish the thought. He didn't need to.

That wouldn't have happened in the early days of pro basketball. Prior to the shot-clock, the "stall" was a key strategy in the game. It accounted for the lowest scoring game in NBA history: November 22, 1950 — the Fort Wayne Pistons edged the Minneapolis Lakers 19-18. While some, like the Celtics Bob Cousy, could entertain with their dribbling and ball-handling prowess, the slowness of play was not exciting and fans were dwindling. The only way to counter the stall was to foul the player with the ball. Free throws were even more common in the last quarter back then than in today's close encounters where the final two minutes seem like nothing but fouls, stopping the game every few seconds. In one game in 1954 Syracuse and New York combined for 75 successful free throws but only 34 regular shots! In a play-off game the year before 107 fouls were committed, leading to 130 free throws. Cousy scored 50 points (a play-off record at that time) with 30 from the charity stripe.

After these two seasons the league knew something had to be done. The game was just too dull. The owner of the Syracuse team, Danny Biasone, pulled together 10 players after the end of the 1953-54 season and they experimented with a stopwatch. Biasone's GM, Leo Ferris, took the length of the game (48 minutes or 2,880 seconds) and divided it by the average number of shots taken by both teams during a pro game (120 at that time). Thus the magic number: 24! The shot-clock was tried in the next pre-season exhibitions, after which the NBA board of governors voted for its inclusion in the regular season. College hoops would later adopt the same rule.

The 24-second shot-clock previewed officially on October 30, 1954, and brought immediate excitement to the game. Rochester beat the Celtics 98-95. During that first shot-clock season, teams averaged 93.1 points. The next season the Celtics would average more than 100 points for the entire season. "Pro basketball would not have survived without a clock," said Biasone. In addition to violating the 24-second shot-clock, a team can also lose the ball if they fail to inbound the ball in 5 seconds or get the ball past mid-court in 10 seconds. If a player stands in the lane (the paint area from the free throw line to the boundary under his own basket) for three seconds, the team also loses possession of the ball.

Basketball is a game of seconds. Of course, time is also controlled on the court by the game clock: four 8-minute quarters in high school; two 20-minute halves in college; four 12-minute quarters in pro ball. In case of a tie, the overtime period is 3 minutes for HS and 5 minutes for college and pros. You just hope your team has more points on the scoreboard when time runs out.

Time will run out for all of us someday. Death is a common denominator for everyone. Those of us who believe in Christ will re-unite someday in heaven, but until then we will miss those who go before us.

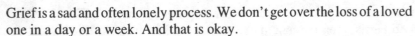

Grief is a sad and often lonely process. We don't get over the loss of a loved one in a day or a week. And that is okay.

The book *Good Grief* briefly explains the stages most people usually go through as they experience loss. For some the stages may go in order; for others, they may be shuffled. For most of us, it is a two-steps-forward, one-step-back process (sometimes even one-step-forward, two-back). We begin in a state of shock and move through emotions of depression and loneliness. We may feel physically ill and become panicked with the feeling we are nearly obsessed by thoughts of our loved one. There may even be a sense of guilt, anger, and resentment toward the deceased (and God). We resist returning to a normal life without our loved one. But gradually hope comes through and we struggle to affirm reality. Life will never be quite the same, but it can become a new kind of normal. Seek God in your grieving, for as Jesus himself taught: *"Blessed are those who mourn, for they will be comforted"* (Matt. 5:4).

[Jesus speaking] "I am the resurrection and the life. He who believes in me will live, even though he dies; and whoever lives and believes in me will never die" (John 11:25).

"With the [shot] clock, we have constant action. I think it saved the game . . . it allowed the game to breathe and progress." — Bob Cousy (Hall of Fame 1970)

Like Father, Like Son

"Any son or daughter whose dad was a coach is a good free-throw shooter," says former coach-turned-analyst Al McGuire, "because they spent time in the gym and on blacktops at camps with their dad from the time they were little." McGuire ought to know. His son Allie even played for him at Marquette University.

Charlie Ward (football's Heisman trophy winner at Florida State and now a guard for the NY Knicks) was coached by his dad (Charles Sr.) in both sports at Central High in Thomasville, Georgia. The Knicks guard credits his dad (both parents) for the solid direction that has made him a success. Among other pro players whose dad also wore the title "Coach" are John Stockton, Rex Chapman, Travis Ford, Bobby Hurley, and Jay Burson.

Head coach at the University of Cincinnati, Bob Huggins also played for his dad. "A lot of my coaching style, I took from him," says Huggins who is known for being tough on his players. "My dad always felt he had to be hard on you in practice. . . . With him, you were prepared to beat the best. He got on us, but he did it the right way . . . he didn't have to use four letter words to get on us," says the Bearcat coach known for his courtside histrionics.

Steve Alford (Indiana 1987 and 4-year NBA veteran) played for his dad in high school, too. Now the head coach at Missouri State, Alford asked his father to be one of his assistants. "The only time he calls me Dad these days," says Sam Alford, "is when he needs a baby sitter."

Rick Barry was too busy playing professional basketball himself to coach his sons, but both Jon (Bucks) and Brent (Clippers) have had to live up to Dad's basketball reputation. Brent won the 1996 All Star Slam-Dunk contest. Younger brother Drew plays for Georgia Tech with still one more Barry playing hoops at the high school level. Another current college hoopster is LSU's Adam Walton, son of former NBA star Bill Walton. Another son, Nate, will attend Princeton starting in 1996-97.

While his father did not coach him nor play basketball before him, Grant Hill, nonetheless, has lived under the spotlight of a dad in professional sports. However, Yale graduate and former NFL Cowboy Calvin Hill (along with Grant's mom) stressed getting a good education and being well-rounded. "I think they had expectations for me, but not in sports," says the Duke graduate who also plays piano. "I think if anything, my parents tried to avoid that. They know how hard it can be for kids of famous parents." Hill has one of the most squeaky clean images in the game today and a personality that wins everyone who meets him. He was Co-Rookie of the year (with Jason Kidd) in 1995 and led the league in the All Star balloting in both 1995-96. His coach with the Pistons is Doug Collins, who is the father of former Duke teammate Chris. It seems the father-son connections never stop.

San Antonio Spur star David Robinson is learning still another part of the equation. Father of two small sons himself, Robinson says of David Jr., "He's like a mirror image of me, and I feel such a tremendous responsibility because he doesn't know anything. I look at him and say, 'Son I have a lot for you. Right now you're not ready for it. But when you mature, I have such great things.' It really gives me an understanding of how God looks at me." Robinson says he now better understands just how much God loves him and has in store for him if only he will listen and learn. He says, "I've probably learned as much about God through my son as any experience I've ever had."

Father — Son — and Holy Spirit. God is there for each of us — to lead us when He knows we are ready. We only need to listen and be willing to learn!

"The father of a righteous man has great joy; he who has a wise son delights in him" (Prov. 23:24).

"You never want to push your children into anything. To me, just try to give them the opportunities to hopefully find something in their life that will give them as much joy — whether basketball, business, music — whatever." — Bill Walton (1992 Hall Of Fame)

Lesson 27
Transition

Wilt Chamberlain and Bill Russell defined the word "rebound" in NBA basketball. The only two players to grab more than 20,000 career rebounds (Chamberlain 23,924; Russell 21,620), more than 2,000 in a single season (C - 2,149; R - 2052), and more than 50 in a single game (C - 55; R - 51), it's no wonder fans were mesmerized by the court action when these two were rivals in the 1960s.

"Fifty in a single game" is the goal of the leading rebounder in the NBA today — Dennis Rodman. Known as much for the wacky color and designs of his hair, and his nose and earrings, Rodman's rebounding ability is not even closely challenged. During the 1994-95 season, he averaged 16.8 rebounds per game. Dikembe Mutombo was second with 12.5. While not a role model for young people in most of his on and off-court antics, Rodman still sets the standards for rebounding. The wild-mannered player says he wants people to see rebounding as an art, "a form that's just like scoring."

Rodman spends hours analyzing tapes. Says former Spurs teammate Jack Haley, "He compares himself to a computer. The hardware is his body, which he keeps in peak physical shape, and the software is his knowledge, what he knows about different shooters' tendencies and how shots from certain spots on the floor tend to come off the rim." He has learned that flat shots tend to come back straight and more quickly. High arcs tend to stay closer to the rim — going either straight up or off the opposite side. If either Jordan or Pippen (his current teammates) shoot from the top of the arc, Rodman has learned these shots usually rebound to the right.

Rodman positions himself for each rebound, often in uncontested areas. "While most guys turn and watch the rim waiting for the ball to come off," Rodman says his secret is "I watch the ball in the air and make adjustments."

Another dimension of his rebounding is his ability to start the transition — to spot the open player and make a spectacular pass for the fast break. Transition is the part of the game that changes quickly from defense to offense or vice versa. The fast break does not allow the other team to double up the player with the ball. With teammates like Pippen, Jordan, and Kukoc, this transition game can be a most successful weapon for the Bulls.

Transition is also a part of success in our personal lives. Transition, simply defined, means change. Life is filled with changes. We can't stop them if we want to, but we can anticipate some of the difficult changes and put ourselves (and loved ones) in the best position to handle them.

Transitions that seem to affect people most are: relocating (moving from one city to another); growing up (which begins with adolescence and ends with leaving home for college/job or moving into your own place); marriage and becoming a parent; and midlife and the "empty nest" (when kids leave home). Growing old (including retirement and death — your parents' and friends' and preparing for your own) often initiates a major transition in our lives.

The book *Transitions — Savoring the Seasons of Life* makes suggestions for all of the above periods. We need to build a support group for ourselves. Certainly this includes our spouse and family, but we need to reach out further. We need close friends with whom we can share. We need Christian friends who will pray for us and hold us accountable during the tough times. If you move to a new town, find a church as soon as you arrive. This is the best place to quickly establish the kind of new friends who will mean the most to you and your family. Seek out the pastor and see if there is a support group in the area if you are having an extremely difficult time. There are others who face the same transitions or changes that you do. Reaching out will not only help you through this difficult time, but may rescue another person as well. Of course, Bible study and prayer are keys in transition survival. No matter where we are or what changes may be taking place in our lives, God is always there to listen to us and guide us.

"Jesus Christ is the same yesterday and today and forever" (Heb. 13:8).

"Even if Rodman guesses wrong, he has the ability to adjust quickly. Most guys are straight-up jumpers, but Dennis can adjust his body in the air to get to a ball." — Johnny "Red" Kerr (Bulls broadcaster who averaged in double figures himself in the '50s-'60s)

Lesson 28
Leaving a Legacy

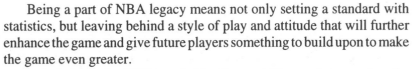

Being a part of NBA legacy means not only setting a standard with statistics, but leaving behind a style of play and attitude that will further enhance the game and give future players something to build upon to make the game even greater.

In its infancy the NBA was led by George Mikan, who passed on the center post to Wilt Chamberlain and Bill Russell, who pushed each other to establish records still intact today. Kareem Abdul-Jabbar extended the finesse of the position with his famous "sky hook" shot copied by younger players. From Kareem to Hakeem, Olajuwon has added quickness to the strength and power of the post position. Other younger centers like Shaquille O'Neal will contribute to the legacy at center as well.

Bob Cousy set the stage for Oscar Robertson at guard. "The Big O" to his fans, Robertson dominated the game. Former teammate Jerry Lucas said, "He was unbelievable, way ahead of his time. There is no more complete player than Oscar." In his second year in the league, he became the only player in history to average a triple-double: 30.8 points, 12.5 rebounds, and 11.4 assists. That same year two-year-old Earvin Johnson began dribbling a basketball. By the time he graduated from Michigan State, "Magic" was already destined to be an NBA legend. Said former teammate James Worthy, "There'll never be another 6'9" point guard that smiles when he humiliates you." With some Magic of his own in Orlando, Penny Hardaway is the heir apparent. He understands "Magic and Oscar, even though they were known as great players, were known for winning. I hope I leave the impression that I knew how to win."

Winning with drama is how great "clutch" shooters will be remembered. "Mr. Clutch", Jerry West, said of himself: "When we were in a time-out, I didn't want a play to be called — just give me the ball and let me see what I can do." Larry Bird expressed the same sentiments during time-outs, "Coach, uh, just give me the ball and tell everybody else to get out of my way." While Nick Van Exel hits unbelievable clutch shots (including one in the Lakers' win to close out Bird's old Boston Gardens), most people feel the player most likely to carry this torch is Reggie Miller. When the game is on the line, Reggie wants the ball. "Everyone knows where the ball is going to end up, and there's nothing that no one else can do about it."

There's nothing anyone can say to fully describe the qualities of the greatest all-time legends. Robertson was certainly one. So was Dr. J. And then there's Michael. Julius (Dr. J) Erving brought creativity, finesse, and a flashy style that put a new face on the game of basketball. Youngsters everywhere began practicing 360's and windmill jams. Michael Jordan picked up where the good doctor left off. Others may have similar moves but MJ's grace and "hang time" combine for innovations often beyond belief. The other qualities these three offer are their love of the game's heritage and their dreams for its future. They have character and class and are positive role models — both on and off the court. They are true ambassadors of basketball. Most people (including these legends themselves) feel Grant Hill will be the next great ambassador. He has the class and commitment to higher ideals. He is gracious with fans and media, respectful of officials and other players, and seems to understand what the word legacy truly means.

We each will leave behind footsteps for others to follow — our children, students, players, and friends? What kind of appreciation for life do they see in us? To what do they see we are committed? The most important heritage we can leave is our faith. While each one who follows us must accept Christ for himself or herself, we can let them see (and hear) what knowing and loving Jesus means to us. When our time on earth is over (and we never know at what moment that might be), the greatest peace we can give our family and friends as they grieve is that we have committed our life to Christ and will one day see them again. What is your legacy?

"Your statutes are my heritage forever; they are the joy of my heart" (Ps. 119:111).

"The true measure of their greatness can only be found in their reflection of each other." — Hal Douglas (narrator, NBA Legacy Video — talking about Magic Johnson and Larry Bird, but it applies to all legends)

Lesson 29
Origin of the Game

In December of 1891 the phys ed instructor at a YMCA school in Springfield, Massachusetts, James Naismith, was asked to create a new indoor activity. The 30-year-old Canadian (also an ordained minister) combined aspects of lacrosse, rugby, soccer, and hockey. The janitor, Pop Stebbins, nailed two peach baskets to the balcony at either end of the gymnasium for goals. Naismith had 13 basic rules, used a soccer ball, and started with nine players on each team. They could pass or bounce the ball to a teammate, but they could not run with it. Only one basket was scored in that first game, by William R. Chase. Dribbling was later added as an option and the number of players per team changed to five.

In the early years, to protect players (and officials) from rowdy fans, wire cages were often built around the court. Thus, players were known as "cagers." Due to injuries from running into the wires, the cages were replaced with nets and eventually discarded altogether. Basketball became a popular outdoor sport as well. High schools and colleges incorporated basketball into their programs. U.S. servicemen carried the game overseas and it became an Olympic sport in 1936.

Abe Saperstein put together the first Harlem Globetrotter team in 1927, but professional basketball was basically unsuccessful until the 1940s. Several hockey team owners wanted to fill open dates in their arenas. Enlisting the help of Ned Irish, who had popularized college matches at Madison Square Gardens, they established the

Basketball Association of America with 11 franchises. The first game was played on November 1, 1946, between the Toronto Huskies and the New York Knickerbockers. A similar group formed in the Midwest and three years later the two organizations joined as the National Basketball League, eventually reorganizing as the National Basketball Association.

In 1967 the American Basketball Association was formed with Hall of Famer (1959) George Mikan serving as commissioner. They focused more on merchandising and entertainment, bringing the slam-dunk and three-point shot to add excitement to the game. Red, white, and blue balls added a patriotic appeal and could be followed more easily by television viewers. NBA player Rick Barry jumped to the new league signing with the Oakland Oaks (owned by popular singer Pat Boone). Electrifying audiences as one of the emerging stars with his slam-dunks was the young Julius Erving (later known as Dr. J.).

In 1976 NBA Commissioner Larry O'Brien negotiated bringing the Denver Nuggets, New York Nets, San Antonio Spurs, and Indiana Pacers into the NBA. This basically dissolved the ABA, but some other teams were eventually absorbed as new NBA franchises as well.

While the game has evolved with changes in the rules, height of the basket rim, time limits, the 3-point line, marketing, etc., most people agree that the basics of the game remain the same.

There is much disagreement, however, about whether or not man himself evolved. Believers in evolution and creationists have been battling for decades. In 1925 high school teacher John Scopes was banned for teaching Darwin's evolution. After the Supreme Court later ruled that ban

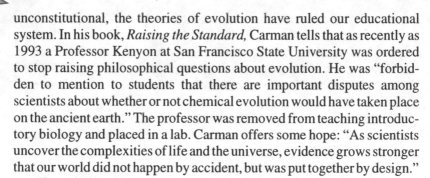

unconstitutional, the theories of evolution have ruled our educational system. In his book, *Raising the Standard,* Carman tells that as recently as 1993 a Professor Kenyon at San Francisco State University was ordered to stop raising philosophical questions about evolution. He was "forbidden to mention to students that there are important disputes among scientists about whether or not chemical evolution would have taken place on the ancient earth." The professor was removed from teaching introductory biology and placed in a lab. Carman offers some hope: "As scientists uncover the complexities of life and the universe, evidence grows stronger that our world did not happen by accident, but was put together by design."

If you follow the evolutionist theory back to a single cell, the question still remains: "Where did that cell come from?" God, our Creator, began the process. Indeed, we all did come from One Being.

"In the beginning God created the heavens and the earth. . . . Then God said, 'Let us make man in our own image' " (Gen. 1:1, 26).

"Dr. James Naismith wanted to invent a game that would provide a means to lead young men to Christ. Through such groups [as Athletes in Action and Jammin' Against the Darkness] that vision is being shared as the tool Naismith had in mind." — Dr. Tony Ladd (Wheaton College sports historian)

Lesson 30
Endurance

During the first nine games of the 1995 play-off series, Laker point guard Nick Van Exel played 417 of the possible 442 minutes. He played all 53 minutes of Game 5 in the series with the Spurs. It was Van Exel's 3-point clutch shot with 10 seconds left that tied the game at 88-88. Another of his 3-point launches won the game, 98-96.

A player must be in good shape for such endurance — in individual games and for a long career in the NBA. Randy Smith, who played in the 1970s with Buffalo, San Diego, Cleveland, New York, and Atlanta, holds the career record for consecutive games played, with 906. On pace to overtake Smith in this Cal Ripken category is A.C. Green of the Phoenix Suns. He will be well over the 800 mark at the end of the 1995-96 season, closing in on Johnny "Red" Kerr's second place of 844. (Kerr played for Syracuse and Philadelphia and is now the Bulls announcer.) Green proved his Iron Man endurance when he had two teeth knocked out (by J.R. Reid). While Reid was suspended for two games for the flagrant behavior, Green played the next night using a special mouth guard.

Many players have extended their NBA careers by moving into lesser roles. Wilt Chamberlain (who holds the NBA career record for minutes per game played at 45.6) began playing every minute of every game with Philadelphia, but was more limited in his final seasons with the Lakers. Another Laker star, Kareem Jabbar, played until he was 42.

Endurance is an issue for all of us regardless of age. Often driven by the "more is better" philosophy of modern society, we can easily burn out if we are not careful. We put in too many overtime hours at work and try to serve on too many committees. We try to live up to the role of Super-Dad, Super-Mom, or Super-Spouse.

Many doctors and counselors are treating patients of varying ages for physical and emotional symptoms of burnout. Even our children have schedules that are overloaded. Scads of books on burnout can be found on the psychology shelves of most bookstores.

The Minirth-Meier team from the New Life Clinics give the following suggestions to help deal with the stresses of burnout. We need to keep a proper balance in our lives. Stay in good physical shape. This means regular exercise, proper diet, and adequate rest. Learn to express your feelings. "Base your self-worth on who you are, not what you do." Having good working relationships and a group of trusted friends you can share with is important. Know your limitations. Learn to say "No."

They also suggest an attitude of humility. Learn to depend on God and spend daily quiet time with Him. We are told that Jesus grew "in wisdom and in stature and in favor with God and man" (Luke 2:52). Likewise, if we can balance our lives intellectually, physically, spiritually, and so-cially, we will be better able to avoid the pitfalls of burnout.

"We continually remember . . . your work produced by faith, your labor prompted by love, and your endurance inspired by hope in our Lord Jesus Christ" (1 Thess. 1:3).

 "An NBA season is a marathon, not a sprint." — Jerry West (Hall of Fame 1979)

100

Sources and Recommended Reading

In accordance with copyright laws, all quotes are brief enough in nature and not in competition with any of the following texts and sources that written permission was not necessary. However, we do wish to acknowledge these authors and individuals and encourage you to purchase the books, etc. for further reading.

Allender, Dr. Dan B., *The Wounded Heart* (Colorado Springs, CO: Navpress, 1990).

Alta Vista. Digital Equipment Corporation, 1996.

Athletes in Action, P.O. Box 588, Kings Dominion, Lebanon, OH 45036, (513) 933-2421.

Athlon Sports College Basketball (Nashville, TN: Athlon Sports, 1995-96), "The General" by Bill Benner; "Tournament of Champions" by Mike DeCourcy; "Athlon's 1995-96 Women's Basketball" by Mel Greenburg; "NBA-13, NCAA-0" by David Jones.

Athlon Sports Pro Basketball (Nashville, TN: Athlon Sports, 1995-96), "The Power of Jordan" by Dan Garcia; "Who's the Smartest Guy in the NBA?" by Dave Kreiger; "Special Q&A with Bill Walton" by Dan Shaughnessy; Treatman, Jeremy. "Legacies of the ABA" by Jeremy Treatman; "NBA's Best" by Rick Weinberg.

Bentz, Rob, "The Admiral," *Sports Spectrum*, May 1994.

Bentz, Rob, "A Place in the Sun," *Sports Spectrum*, June 1995.

Bentz, Rob, "The Lights Burn Brightly," *Sports Spectrum*, July 1995.

Branon, Dave, "Don't Read My Lips," *Sports Spectrum*, December 1993.

Branon, Dave, "Point Man," *Sports Spectrum*, December 1993.

Branon, Dave, "Power Forward," *Sports Spectrum*, June 1994.

Callahan, Gerry, "The Worst Kind of Coward," *Sports Illustrated*, 7/31/95.

Carman, *Raising the Standard* (Nashville, TN: Sparrow Press, 1994).

Clark, Jack, "Sports People — Nanci Donnellan," *Sports Illustrated*, 8/1/94.

Complete NBA Basketball (The Ultimate Multimedia Reference), Microsoft Corp., 1994.

Conway, Jim, *Men in Mid-Life Crisis* (Elgin, IL: David C. Cook Publishing, Co., 1978 (22nd printing 1986).

Crouch, Paul, (Bill Bright, editor), "Parting the Sea of Impossibility" *Successful Christian Men Share the Greatest Lesson I've Ever Learned* (San Bernardino, CA: Here's Life Publishers, Inc., 1991).

Dobson, Dr. James, "When God Doesn't Make Sense," audio (Irving, TX: Word, Inc., 1979).

Dr. J's Pro Basketball Yearbook (New York, NY: C.S. Communications, 1995), "Teen Wolf" by Dave Allen; "Power Forwards" by Jim Carty; "Shooting Guards" by Dan Dunkin; "Small Wonder" by Ron

Green; "What's Up Doc?" by Phil Jasner with Julius Erving; "Hurley's Fight Continues" by Martin McNeal; "Point Guards" by Lee Shappell; "Second Coming" by Lyle Spencer; "Nick Van Exel" by Brad Turner; "Jackson Ready for Action" by Richie Whit.

Drollinger, Karen Rudolph, "Legends: Catching Up With . . . Nancy Lieberman-Cline," *Sports Spectrum, June 1994.*

ESPN College Basketball (New York, NY: The Hearst Corp., 1995), "Will There Ever Be Another Fab Five?" by Mitch Alborn; "The Best" by Lee Fitting; "Zooming In" by Roger Jackson; "If John Belushi Were Alive Today, He'd Be Dick Vitale" by Tony Kornheiser; "It's a Whole New Game" by Wendy Parker and Jessie Paolucci; "2 Years Tops . . . or Not Even That Long . . . and Does Anybody Care?" by Jon Pessah; "OK" by Ivan Solotaroff; "Believe It, Baby!" by Dick Vitale.

The ESPY Awards, ESPN, February 1996.

Feinstein, John, "Inside College Basketball — Son Knows Best," *Sports Illustrated*, 1/22/96.

Foster, Richard J., *Money, Sex & Power* (San Francisco, CA: Harper & Row, Publishers, 1985).

Geisler, Dave, "In God He Trusts," *Sports Spectrum*, December 1995.

Geisler, Dave, "The Players' Friend," *Sports Spectrum*, December 1995.

George, Bob, *Classic Christianity* (Eugene, OR: Harvest House Publishers, 1989).

Gerstner, Joanne C., "Lobo, Swoopes Score Marketing Coups," *Cincinnati Enquirer*, Cincinnati, Ohio, 10/28/95.

Global Network Navigator, Inc., "Tara VanDerveer," 1996.

Goshko, John M., "Pope Urges Turn to Spiritual," *Cincinnati Enquirer*, Cincinnati, OH (wire story from the Washington Post), 10/7/95.

Hallford, Curtis, "Medicine Man," *Sports Spectrum*, November 1995.

Hawkins, Don; Frank Minirth; Paul Meier; and Chris Thurman, *Before Burnout* (Chicago, IL: Moody Press, 1990).

Heisler, Mark, "180 Pounds of Attitude," Ultimate Sports Basketball — Pro College Yearbook (Seattle, WA: Ultimate Sports Publishing, Inc., 1995).

Hill, Grant, "Responsibility," *USA Weekend*, 11/17-19/95.

Huggins, Bob and Mike Bass, *Bob Huggins — Pressed for Success* (Champaign, IL: Sagamore Publishing, 1995).

Hunter, Kevin, "Against the Flow," *Sports Spectrum*, December 1995.

Jones, Larry, *Practice to Win* (Wheaton, IL: Tyndale House Publishers, Inc., 1982).

"Just Say No," *48 Hours*, CBS, 2/22/96.

Krzyzewski, Mike, "Keeping in Touch," Sprint Special Advertising Feature, *Sports Illustrated*, 1/29/96.

Leibman, Glenn, *Basketball Shorts* (Chicago, IL: Contemporary Books, 1995).

Lindy's Pro Basketball '95-'96 Annual (Birmingham, AL: D.M.D. Publications, 1995), "Brent Barry Takes the Spotlight" by Scott Howard Cooper; "The Planet Gets the Big Mac" by Jeffrey Denberg; "Keeping the Faith" by Roland Lazenby; "Orlando's Whiz Kids" by Tim Povtak; "The Wolves' New baby Needs No Sitter" by Ray Richardson.

Lynch, Lorrie, "We can't keep waiting," *USA Weekend*, October 22-23, 1995.

McCallum, Jack, "Hoop Dream," *Sports Illustrated*, 6/26/95.

McCartney, Bill, et. al., *Seven Promises of a Promise Keeper* (Colorado Springs, CO: Focus on the Family, 1994).

McGarvey, Robert, "Picture Yourself a Winner," *Reader's Digest* condensed from *Kiwanis*, October 1990.

McGuire, Al, Sports Channel (Warner Cable), University of Cincinnati vs. University of South Florida, 2/4/96.

Menconi, Peter; Richard Peace; and Lyman Coleman, *Transitions — Savoring the Seasons of Life* (Littleton, CO: Serendipity House, 1988).

Minirth, Frank; Paul Meier; and Stephen Arterburn, *The Complete Life Encyclopedia* (Nashville, TN: Thomas Nelson Publishers, 1995).

Montville, Leigh, "Giant," *Sports Illustrated*, 10/2/95.

Myers, Chris with Bill Walton, *Up Close*, ESPN, February 1996.

Nash, Bruce and Allan Zullo, *The Basketball Hall of Shame* (New York, NY: Archway Paperback (Pocket Books), 1991).

NBA 46th Annual All Star Game, NBC Sports, 2/11/96.

NBA Legacy: Living Legends to Rising Stars, NBA Entertainment, Inc. with CBS/FOX (Beverly Hills, CA: FoxVideo, Inc., 1995).

The NBA on TNT, post-game interview (Lakers Game), TNT, 1/30/96.

Ogilvie, Lloyd John, "You Can Depend on Me" *God's Treasury of Virtues* (Tulsa, OK: Honor Books, 1995).

Olson, Brad, "Actively Listening," sermon, Milford United Methodist Church, 7/23/95.

OMS International, Inc., P.O. Box A, Greenwood, IN 46142-6599, 317/881-6751.

Patterson, Leroy, *The Best Is Yet To Be* (Wheaton, IL: Tyndale House Publishers, Inc., 1986).

Pera, Gina, "Most Caring Coaches Award," *USA Weekend*, 1/26-28/96.

"Personal Foul," editorial, *Cincinnati Enquirer*, Cincinnati, OH, 1/29/96.

Petersen's Pro Basketball (Los Angeles, CA: Petersen Publishing Co., 1995), "Q&A: Michael Jordan" by Lacy J. Banks; "Could it be magic?" by Barry Cooper; "NBA Shootaround" by Darryl Howerton; "All Time NBA All Star Team" by Donald Hunt; "King of the Hill" by Jeff Ryan.

Rivers, Glenn "Doc" and Bruce Brooks, *Those Who Love the Game* (New York, NY: Henry Holt & Co., 1993).

Salzberg, Charles, *From Set Shot to Slam Dunk* (New York, NY: E.P. Dutton, 1987).

Seamands, David A., *If Only — Moving Beyond Blame to Belief* (Wheaton, IL: Victor Books, 1995).

SLAM (New York, NY: Harris Publications, November 1995), "The BOMB — Reggie Miller" by Scoop Jackson; "A Love Supreme — Penny Hardaway" by Scoop Jackson; "Biggie Smalls — Muggsy

Bogues" by Vincent M. Mallozzi; "Smooth Operator — Cedric Ceballos" by Jay Richards.

Smalley, Gary, *Hidden Keys to Loving Relationships* (video series), Gary Smalley Seminars, Inc., 1993.

The Sporting News Pro Basketball Yearbook (St. Louis, MO: A Times Mirror Company, 1995), "Thrown to the Wolves" by Steve Aschburner; "He's Still Mr. Clutch" by Mitch Chortkoff; "Adventures in Baby-sitting" by Dave D'Alessandro; "The Man in the Bubble" by Corky Meinecke; "Thanks for the Complement" by Dave Moore; "Scouting the NBA" by Shaun Powell.

SportsLine USA, SportsTicker Enterprises, L.P., 2/20/96.

Sports Machine, CBS Sports (WCPO, TV-9 Cincinnati), 5/21/95.

Storm, Hannah, NBC Sports (Christmas Eve 1995 special — Avery Johnson part of report)

Strand, Robert, "Handicapped," *Moments for Teachers* (Green Forest, AR: New Leaf Press, Inc., 1995).

Sullivan, Tim, "Reggie Puts on a Show," *Cincinnati Enquirer*, Cincinnati, OH, 4/30/95.

Swindoll, Charles R., *Growing Strong in the Seasons of Life* (Portland, OR: Multnomah Press, 1983).

"The Tale of Bob Kurland," A Canon special advertising feature, *Sports Illustrated*, 11/6/95.

Taylor, Phil, cover story, "The Best Rebounder Ever?" *Sports Illustrated*, 3/4/96.

Taylor, Phil, "The Oldest Pick in the Book," *Sports Illustrated*, 11/13/95.

"Upheaval lurks in Hogs' future" Associated Press release, *Cincinnati Enquirer*, Cincinnati, OH, 4/5/95.

The V Foundation and DesigNet @ PRODIGY, 1996.

Walk to Emmaus, "Christian Action and Perseverance Talks," The Upper Room, 1985.

Wangerin, Walter Jr., *Little Lamb, Who Made Thee?* (Grand Rapids, MI: Zondervan Publishing House, 1993).

Web Browser @ PRODIGY, Prodigy Services, 1988-94, Microstar Software Ltd., 1985-1993.

Westburg, Granger E., *Good Grief* (Philadelphia, PA: Fortress Press, 1962, 1971).

Wolff, Alexander, "Living Legends," *Sports Illustrated*, 12/25/95-1/1/96.

Wolff, Alexander and Christian Stone, "Scorecard — Foul-Shooting Most Foul," *Sports Illustrated*, 6/19/95.

Wolff, Alexander and Christian Stone, "Scorecard — Deep Six-on-Sixed," *Sports Illustrated*, 3/20/95.

"Women's Pro Basketball Will Start in Fall," Associated Press, *Cincinnati Enquirer*, Cincinnati, OH, 2/22/96.

Woolwine, Sam, "The Cleveland Connection," *Sports Spectrum*, December 1993.

The World Book Encyclopedia, Volumes 2-B, 6-E, and 14- N/O (Chicago, IL: World Book, Inc. 1983).